PRAISE FOR THE NEW BUSINESS BRIGADE

"A superb book! THE definitive source on the great challenge of our age. After the longest war in American history, a war with aspects that may well continue for decades to come, the defining challenge of our time is to integrate our veterans—this New Greatest Generation—back into the workplace. This book is essential reading for business, for the veterans, for their families, and for anyone who cares about our nation and those who have served our nation in time of war."

Lt. Col. Dave Grossman
Author, *On Combat* and *On Killing*

"The New Business Brigade is a wake-up call for US businesses to finally and fully discover the truly valuable human resource of our military transitioning home. Ubaldi's book opens our eyes to realize not only what our nation's tax dollars have intelligently paid for in defending our country but also the hidden treasure of our veterans' skill, character, and leadership in contributing in a huge way to the economic expansion of our nation.

"John Ubaldi, a 30-year Marine and himself a successful career transitioned vet, has written this very important and timely book that should be read by anyone owning a business looking to hire the best as well as any veteran preparing for or involved in career transition."

Joe Yazbeck
Founder, President, Prestige Leadership Advisors
International Leadership Coach and Speaker
Best-Selling Author, *No Fear Speaking*

"Is there life after war? The question could not be timelier given the recent and projected de-escalation of America's involvement in military conflicts in Iraq and Afghanistan. Since the all-volunteer military was adopted by this country nearly 40 years ago, the issues facing returning veterans in a society that has less and less experience serving in the armed forces have been in increasing contrast with the rest of the nation. In short, the vast majority of citizens and their leaders have little idea what it means to serve.

"An experienced combat veteran in both Iraq and Afghanistan, Ubaldi takes on the issues of returning soldiers from a first-hand point of view while retaining a clear-eyed objectivity of policy implementation. He spends time helping non-military readers dispel the myths associate in popular culture. Is "Post Traumatic Stress Disorder" ubiquitous? Why are veterans having a difficult time finding work at a rate well above the national averages? Do skills acquired in the military translate into real-world benefits to employers?

"The book is part resource and part case study for those who are in human resources, small business, and public policy. It deals bluntly with the benefits and even a few of the liabilities of hiring returning veterans in a way that is well-informed and extremely readable. For those who have served in the military, it is an outstanding orientation of the issues they are facing without indulging in useless self-pity. The book will also help those who love a returning veteran understand what they have faced and may yet confront as they re-enter civilian life.

"I strongly recommend this informative book to veterans, their friends and families, policy makers, and especially those who are interested in building up their businesses with the best trained, best motivated, and most mature men and women their generation has to offer.

Scott McDonald
McDonald & Associates

"This is a GREAT book and should be read by all those in civilian leadership. Many times the civilian leadership does not understand what we in the military have gone through and the challenges we face once we are released back into the civilian workforce. I am an example of this book and civilian leadership not understanding what I have gone through. Being a retired Gunnery Sergeant, I believe that I was released from my recent job for being a self-starter, and go-getter. Marine Leadership is taught to lead from the front and set the example. Many civilian employers feel threatened by this since they have never been in our boots. Thank you MGySgt Ubaldi for bring this book to light and I hope it will be one that is issued to all civilian leadership. You hit the nail on the head with this one. Semper Fi!"

GySgt Jack Williams
United States Marine Corps Retired

"I anchor an afternoon news show in Sacramento, and John Ubaldi was our go-to military expert for many years. We always appreciated his candid and thoughtful perspective from someone who had actually served in the conflicts he reported on. He gave us insight other so-called "experts" couldn't provide because he had actual boots on the ground experience.

"With his book, The New Business Brigade, Ubaldi brings his common sense approach to the issue of putting veterans to work as he underscores the mutual benefits to employer and employee. The special qualities of a veteran, gained only by the experience of serving our country in the manner in which they do, are spotlighted and explored while illustrating the resulting enhancement they bring to business and society.

"Ubaldi is true advocate and voice for veterans, as well as a patriot."

Kitty O'Neal
Sacramento, California Radio Personality, KFBK Radio 1530AM

"Every man or woman who enters the military should read this book beginning on day one. Business leaders must embrace the principles that Ubaldi hammers home on each page. Every politician can learn their duty and obligation to the women and men who have, do and will serve in our armed forces. Mr. Ubaldi brings to the clear light of day the vast resources and strengths that are typified by our military vets. As an educator I understand the great potential of those who serve and the need for the re-education of America. This book is the beginning of that education."

Kelly Timpson
Public School Educator

"This book informs the returning service man how to market his unique training so an employer knows his exceptional value. Military friendly businesses and colleges are listed. A business owner is made aware of the potentially great asset a vet hire can be to him."

Capt Richard Stoeltzing
U.S. Navy Retired

"Great Read . . . I only wish i could send a copy to every business leader and media executive so that they can understand that not every veteran is crazy and that not every veteran with PTSD is a murderer. This book also sheds some light on the fact that your best employees are and can be those veterans with skills sets that is so missing in today's business environment. Those skills are true leadership that understands how to make decisions and stand by them. Also the ability to be a forward thinker and layout plans and contingencies just in case plan A isn't exactly perfect. It's also a good book for veterans to read so that they understand that they aren't alone in this fight to integrate back into corporate America. And if they choose to start their own business that there is help out there from people that understand. Semper Fidelis"

MGySgt Mark Kline
United States Marine Corps Retired

"As a current member of the Army looking at the end of my career in the next few years, this book really relates to some of the challenges that we are facing as veterans. With over 20 years of service, I do not have any "civilian" work experience, so John Ubaldi really has a way of identifying those challenging areas and comes up with creative recommendations for the veteran. I highly recommend this book to veterans and service members before they get out of the service.

"This book is also a must read for employers. Employers need to understand that there is a potential work force out there of veterans who have values that will be beneficial for their company.

"Overall this is an excellent book, well written, and relevant on multiple levels."

Capt John Belisle
United States Army

"Having studied Political Science and International Relations for some time, this is the first book I have come across that delves into a controversial, yet very relevant topic: life after war and the effect on the US market via American veterans. Both civilians and veterans alike can gain a more realistic perspective on what John Ubaldi adequately refers to as America's 'untapped resource', the U.S. Veteran."

Sabrina Moreno
Veteran United States Marine Corps

"Good read. It gives a good perspective on the valuable resource that exists in our veterans, and the challenges facing them as they integrate back into the workforce. I particularly enjoyed the use of the sheepdog analogy as guardians of the nation, and the influence and example they provide for all of us. You will enjoy very much the discussions of leadership and the impact that it can have in successful business relationships with veterans.

"As a member of the US Coast Guard Auxiliary I see many of the values spoken of in this book as I work with several veterans that volunteer in our program, and I would recommend it to friends and family, as well as anyone in the workforce looking for value, loyalty, and devotion to duty. It sheds a bright light on some of our nation's finest gems...may they sparkle for all to see and enjoy."

John Kennedy
Kennedy Consulting

"This book opened my eyes and made me aware of the things I had no idea the majority of veterans go through. The 99% of us who are not veterans need to understand how this 1% is impacting our current lives in ways we have never thought about before.

"The book tells Human Resources staff on the private or public sector how to benefit from hiring veterans. Ubaldi gets you the actual veteran's statistics, no media manipulating reports that all they do is thwart the truth on these valuable beings.

"When I finished reading the book, I was able to better understand how much positive contribution and results a veteran could bring to any company.

"Also, I found this to be especially useful for those who have retired as veterans or are about to retire from active duty and want to be absorbed into the normal day to day business life. The value of the book is that it provides specific steps to take as a veteran, especially if you are thinking on starting you own business. You will probably benefit a lot with this quick and easy to understand reading.

"For me, there is no better way to help a veteran than to understand his or her life as a soldier, and to know all the enormous value he or she can give to society, after coming back home. That's why I purchased this book."

Sergio Rodriguez
Owner of Advanced Marketing

"The Author is definitely a scholar as pertain to Veteran Culture, nonetheless the American Public have a long way to go before they understand what American Veterans are all about. Thank you."

Dr. Bob Hollis
President, Vet to Vet Advocate

"Excellent book written in a clear and concise manner; good read."

Junior Delgiorno
U.S. Navy Veteran

"This book was an easy read and covered a wide range of topics that veterans face today. It also covers many topics that employers and the public generally don't think about when it comes to veterans. It gives a good perspective on how employers under value the military veteran's they hire. The book covers a wide range of relevant topics that were thoroughly researched and made clear easy points to understand. This book should be recommended to anyone involved in a company's hiring process and a great read for manager's/ supervisor's whom have veterans on their teams.

"Personally being a veteran and having served it made me realize that I unintentionally omitted much of my responsibilities in the military because I did not feel they would translate well into a civilian sector job. After reading this book I have begun the process of editing my resume."

Danny Perez
Veteran of the United States Marine Corps

"John Ubaldi offers specific examples of how transitioning veterans contribute their skills and ideas in today's workplace. Key to success will be finding ways to get through corporate HR and hiring practices to identify career opportunities that can effectively utilize their unique capabilities. With Florida's commitment to be the #1 location for veteran employment, the state must continue to expand in aviation, logistics and global trade to create a dynamic business environment."

Jenny Clark
CEO of Solvability

"Outstanding! Well-constructed, well-written, and easily understood. Extremely well researched and presented, providing veterans the tools to an easier transition, with dignity & purpose."

Shelly Bauer
President of Universal Investigations, LLC

"I'm not a service person, but I have always appreciated the efforts of their service during war and during peace. John has really brought an entirely new point of view. I appreciated reading this book and look forward to reading more from him. I'm so grateful for the service men and women! Thank you for keeping the U.S. free."

Katherine Beus-Cusumano
Family Community Organizer

"This book provides easy to understand awareness related to the struggles of our US Vets returning to the private sectors and enlightened me on how to help and be an advocate, promoter and supporter to all those who fight selflessly to defend our country."

Janine Vassall
Director of Volunteer Services
Community Learning Center of Clearwater, Florida

"Hurrah for John Ubaldi. This is a book that should be read by all return veterans. a great help ! Listen to someone who has experienced what most veterans are quiet to talk about. Lots of good information on the history of our country and the involvements they have been in to keep freedom for us all.

"A must read for anyone!"

Nicki Larson
Business Owner/ Travel Consultant

"John Ubaldi of UbaldiReports.com addresses a timely topic in his book, The New Business Brigade, Veterans' Dynamic Impact on US Business. He writes that veterans have even greater disadvantages in the already poor job market where full employment remains elusive. He clearly sets out the primary problems confronting returning veterans in today's economy and makes powerful arguments to employers about the mistake of disregarding the skills built by veterans during their military experience. For the returning veteran, Ubaldi identifies ways of using operational and organizational skills acquired during active duty. He identifies federal opportunities and programs of particular interest to veterans and. suggests that returning veterans make good use of the alliances and friendships developed during service, especially when seeking out mentors and new opportunities.

"While we applaud our veterans for their service they are not necessarily welcomed to the workplace. The public's perception of the returning veteran is limited by the public's lack of understanding of military life. Ubaldi outlines the marketable skills built by military service and reminds us that while some returning veterans have traumatic issues that are in the forefront of daily news, the vast majority are healthy, skilled and well-prepared to take on today's workplace. They are eager and willing to apply the lessons learned in the military to post military life. He attributes their workplace disadvantage to this lack of understanding of the positive attributes of the military experience but also to the lack of transferable certification for work training acquired in the military.

"In reading this book, I realized how my perceptions of the military were formed more by media reports than by real understanding of what a soldier does within the military. It opened my eyes to how useful military skill building can be once military service concludes. I would recommend this book to both employers and returning veterans."

Nancy Mullen
Community Advocate

THE NEW BUSINESS
BRIGADE

THE NEW BUSINESS
BRIGADE

Veterans' Dynamic Impact on US Business

JOHN UBALDI

DocUmeant *Publishing*
244 5th Avenue
Suite G-200
NY, NY 10001
646-233-4366
www.DocUmeantPublishing.com

Published by
DocUmeant Publishing
244 5th Avenue, Suite G-200
New York, NY 10001

For permission or bulk orders contact:

DocUmeant Publishing
244 5th Avenue, Suite G-200, NY, NY 10001
646-233-4366 • Direct 727-565-2130

publisher@documeantpublishing.com

Copy Editor, Philip S Marks

Asst. Copy Editor, Gary Ciesla

Cover and layout, DocUmeant Designs
http://www.DocUmeantDesigns.com

Library of Congress Control Number: 2014957466

Ubaldi, John
    The New Business Brigade: Veterans Dynamic Impact on US Business / by John Ubaldi -- 1st ed.
    p. cm.

    1. Community reintegration, Veteran ; Post-deployment reintegration ; Reintegration, Veteran ; Veteran-community reintegration ; Veterans--Reintegration. 2. Business & Economics--Labor & Industrial Relations. I. Title.

ISBN: 978-1-937801-50-2

DEDICATION

This book is dedicated to all the men and women who served in the armed forces whether in peacetime or war. You gave something of yourselves for your country and for the freedom we enjoy.

CONTENTS

FOREWORD

Master Gunny Ubaldi, as I call him, was and is a great US Marine enlisted leader that worked with me at our base at Camp Pendleton, California, and in Afghanistan and Iraq, in the Global War on Terror. He was not only a great leader of men and women, but he was one of a rare group of military leaders that I always said that has the "critical thinking skills to resolve complex problems in a gray and uncertain world". He is a big thinker and the world needs more of these thinkers with the moral courage to say what needs to be said with a bevy of solutions to accompany the challenges that he outlines in this book.

John Ubaldi has hit on a nerve that those of us that have served in the military, and have been on the battlefields of America and the world, have been trying to communicate to those we have protected and to those capitalists who hire talent, and fail to understand the talent military men and women bring to non-military organizations. This is an essential read for those that want to understand this problem, and understand it is about the 21 million plus veterans in America.

Ubaldi, a combat veteran of Afghanistan and Iraq, has described the challenges he and other combat veterans experience by civilians of acceptance or non-acceptance for veterans, both for their military combat service for the people of America and our allies, and their eventual return and recovery to civilian life.

Many are concerned about the effects of PTS (Post Traumatic Stress). It is about stress recovery, and it is not a "Disorder" as has been described by many. Ubaldi describes his "long walk home" in this process and overcoming stigmas that those who do not understand the military training and ethos fail to understand or recognize.

Because of his experiences, Ubaldi discusses his need to set up a "Veterans Transition Academy". He describes this need due to the weakness and the lack of reality in the transition programs in the military. Poor hand offs between the Department of Defense to the Department of Veterans Affairs, and onto the educational and employment markets. Veterans need translation and mentorship on both sides of their experiences. I have described this during my experience with all my veteran leadership as "stay in in their faces". To be successful either in fighting the enemy or winning the battles at home, someone, a mentor that understands, is needed to guide the veteran too success. Ubaldi does this in his book and helps the diaspora in this discussion and how to do about it.

He describes throughout the book ways to succeed, whether as a veteran, as an educator, as an individual who wants to help veterans, or as a business that wants to hire veterans. Additionally, he discussed the challenges with the Department of Veterans Affairs experience and process. This is an area where much more education is required while in military service, in transition of military service, and post-military service. Ubaldi makes solid recommendations to resolve this challenge for veterans and their families. Veterans have left much money on the table because they and their families fail to understand this process. One cannot give up because the bureaucracy of the VA is challenging.

Ubaldi provides an extensive analysis of the issues in Post-Traumatic Stress. Commonly known as PTSD, this is really not a disorder, but he describes the experiences combat veterans deal with personally, in clinical experiences, and dealings with the public at-large.

He goes on to describe the special challenges of the Reserve and National Guard forces assigned to active duty and the challenging experiences of this class of military service. He describes the "second class" status the Department of Defense and Congress has relegated to these great Americans. Although, Ubaldi gives a great account of the experiences of the reserve and guard forces, he does not cover an essential discussion about how Federal statutes Title 10, Title 32, and Title 50 that cover the funding of the active forces, reserves, and guard forces. These statutes need to be normalized for funding and benefits. The debate needs to be held because of the changing face of warfare and needs of the veterans and their families.

Ubaldi concludes this work by reviewing the challenges in Washington, DC, and with the political view of veterans and the fact that words are weaker than their actions with veterans, although, things are improving in awareness and actions for veteran's enhanced benefits. Finally, he discusses a plan for a "Call to Action" to ensure that America's veterans and their families are appropriately cared for. This work is sure to educate the reader on the current military experience.

James L. Williams, Major General
US Marine Corps (retired)

PREFACE

Lieutenant General John Kelly spoke to the Semper Fi Society of St. Louis on November 13, 2010, several days after finding out his son, Marine 1st Lieutenant Robert Kelly, had been killed in action in Afghanistan:

"Our country today is in a life and death struggle against an evil enemy, but America as a whole is certainly not at war—not as a country, not as a people. Today only a tiny fraction of American families (less than 1%) shoulder the burden of fear and sacrifice, and they shoulder it for the entire nation. Their sons and daughters who serve are men and women of character who continue to believe in this country enough to put life and limb on the line without qualification and without thought of personal gain, so the sons and daughters of the other 99% don't have to. No big deal though. Marines have always been first to fight—paying in full the bill that comes with being free for everyone else." (Fraser 2010)

The conflict in Iraq and soon the war in Afghanistan will begin to recede into history, only to be remembered by the military personnel who served there. As the veterans return from these conflicts, they return to a different kind of America. They return to a country that barely understood the conflicts they had engaged in, far removed from the self-sacrifice of the generation of Americans who went off to war after the Japanese attack on Pearl Harbor on December 7, 1941.

The Greatest Generation

The attack on Pearl Harbor was a transformational event for the US, as a generation of Americans who had suffered through the Great Depression came of age during the Second World War to liberate a suffering humanity; they returned home to transform America. Over 16 million men and women answered the call of duty, as the entire nation was galvanized for one singular purpose—the defeat of the Axis Alliance.

In his book, *The Greatest Generation,* Tom Brokaw chronicles the stories of these men and women. Brokaw goes out into America to tell the stories of individual men and women, the stories of a generation of American-citizen heroes and heroines who came of age during the Great Depression and the Second World War and then went on to build modern America.

Tom Brokaw was quoted as saying, "They answered the call to save the world from the two most powerful and ruthless military machines ever assembled—instruments of conquest in the hands of fascist maniacs." They faced great odds and a late start, but they did not protest. They succeeded on every front. And as they now reach the twilight of their adventurous and productive lives, they remain, for the most part, exceptionally modest. In a deep sense, they did not think what they were doing was that special because everyone else was doing it too." (Chaplain 2010)

The Next Greatest Generation

Decades later, a similar pivotal event, equally as transformational as the attack on Pearl Harbor occurred. On September 11, 2001, four planes were hijacked, two of the four planes slammed into the World Trade Center in New York and one into the Pentagon. The final plane was brought down by the passengers on board—crashing near Shanksville, PA.

The nation was mesmerized by the tragedy of that day. Unlike the WWII generation, only those who served in the military or chose to join afterward would find themselves fighting in the deserts of Iraq or the mountains of Afghanistan. America has changed dramatically since the Second World War. After the turbulent conflict in Vietnam, the nation adopted an all-volunteer military force. Forty years have passed since the termination of the draft, and few Americans have any real knowledge or connection to those serving in the armed forces. As the conflicts in Iraq and Afghanistan wind down and the armed forces reduce their manpower, we are seeing more veterans entering the workforce. Unlike past conflicts, the vast majority of society has little connection to those serving in the military. How do we integrate veterans back into civilian society in a way that their skills, talents, and experiences can be best applied for the benefit of veterans and society? How do we do this as a nation, when so many Americans are unaware of their sacrifices?

In his book, former Secretary of Defense, Robert Gates wrote, "Most of the public attention with regard to the men and women in uniform seems to fall to one end of the spectrum or the other. The heroes are extolled for their valor and sacrifice. Those who have disgraced the uniform in some way are condemned.

"The latter fortunately are small in number. The former, the heroes, to me are countless. I know that if everyone is a hero then no one truly is. I can see the term is thrown around far too casually. Most troops signed up in a time of war and did their job ably and honorably without fanfare or much recognition. There is no doubt that those who fought bravely, those who saved the lives of their comrades (often at risk of their own), those who were wounded, and those who fell are heroes. How then do you describe the hundreds of thousands who went to Iraq and Afghanistan and did their duty and then returned to their families and must live with the nightmare of war for the rest of their lives? What about the medics, doctors, and nurses who have to deal with so many shattered bodies and minds? Or the aircrews that have been at war since 1991? Or the logistics experts for whom performing miracles became a routine day's work? Or the

Special Forces where 7 or 8 or 10 tours of duty were common? Or all those troops who had to endure fifteen-month tours?

"Wherever I went in the world, these men and women were standing watch for all of us. For some it is a career, for all it is a calling." (Gates 2014)

Sacrificing for a Nation

How do we as a nation welcome these warriors back? How do we put a veteran back to work? Just like the veterans from the greatest generation who transformed this country, the generation that came of age during the attack of September 11, 2001, is now re-entering civilian society to benefit the country they fought so hard to preserve and protect. I myself am one of those returning warriors! Having recently retired as a thirty-year Marine Corps combat vet with three tours of duty in Iraq and Afghanistan, I wanted to do something for all veterans, and this book brings forth the value and the innovation all veterans have ingrained in them.

My own story is no different than the thousands of veterans who were shaped by that fateful day. On September 11, while serving as a Marine Reservist, I was on my way to work at a consulting firm in Sacramento, California, when the first plane slammed into the World Trade Center. By the time I got to work, another plane had crashed into the World Trade Center and then another slammed into the Pentagon, with the final one crashing in Pennsylvania. Viewing the utter destruction that day, I knew the nation was at war!

As soon as I could get to a phone, I called my unit to volunteer for active duty! My request was granted, and I was activated within weeks after the attack. I would then serve two years with a deployment to Afghanistan and spent the first anniversary of the September 11th attack standing in formation at the Bagram Air Force Base in Afghanistan, commemorating that dreadful day.

After being deactivated, I transitioned home, but only for a short period. Within months after I transitioned from active duty to reserve status, I again volunteered to serve, this time in Iraq. I did so even though I didn't have to. I wanted to serve my country, but most importantly, I didn't want to let my fellow Marines down. Many had gone into the breach as they liberated Iraq in 2003. Now it was my turn, from there I was re-activated, and deployed to Ramadi, Iraq in 2005. Upon my return, I went back into active reserve status and returned to the consulting firm I worked at before. Over time, I decided to leave the consulting firm to find other employment, but I had no idea what lay ahead, as soon as I left it became apparent that being a veteran and a reservist was not an asset but a hindrance to finding viable employment.

I had thought it would be no problem to find a job! How wrong I was! There were many obstacles. Many businesses did not want to hire a reservist, they didn't say so outright, but they always asked about my status when they saw on my resume that I was a Marine reservist. They didn't want to hire a reservist because they thought I might have to deploy again to Iraq or Afghanistan. The doors kept shutting on me! So I decided to start my own business. I had no knowledge of how to start a business or what I was going to do, but I knew that I had a natural and passionate interest in politics. So I decided to start a business in it.

In 2009 I developed a website called the "Military Briefing Book." This was a website providing information on national and international topics from a variety of news and media sources which allowed the public to make up their own mind on the issues of the day.

The beginning of my business came at a crucial time. As I was on my way home from Iraq in 2005, I had received a Red Cross message informing me that my mother had passed away. Then I spent the next couple years taking care of my father before he passed away in 2010. In the fall of 2011, I put my business on hold as it was now my turn to deploy again, this time to Afghanistan. I had delayed serving a couple of times because of the health of my father; after his passing I was ready to deploy again to Afghanistan.

It may be hard for most Americans to understand why I would want to deploy to Afghanistan, but I was like thousands of veterans who volunteered to serve in harms' way. Many had their own reasons, but many just did not want to let their comrades down. I was no different; I could not sit idly by as Marines were being deployed to Afghanistan and I remained safe at home. It was my turn to serve—again!

In the fall of 2011 I was re-activated for duty to deploy to Afghanistan in early 2012. When I informed friends and family, to let them know I was deploying to Afghanistan, the mood of the nation was very different than it had been in 2001. All veterans can relate to this experience, as all have experienced this same trend. In 2001, when I volunteered, everyone was proud of my service to my country. Everyone called me a hero for serving our country and continued to do so even when I volunteered for service in Afghanistan in 2002. But when I deployed to Iraq in 2005, the sentiment was dramatically different. Volunteering for Iraq? Everyone kept saying, "Oh, I'm sorry you have to go." That sentiment had changed even further by the time I deployed to Afghanistan in 2012. People asked, "Why are we there?" "Why shouldn't we take care of our own country?"

How does it make you feel when you know the country says they support your mission but then in the same breath they say we just do not support the mission you have been called to do?

The Long Walk Home

After being deactivated in 2012 and returning home, I went a full year before I met anyone who served in Iraq or Afghanistan.

Now that I was home I decided to restart my business, but I was unsure how to re-establish it since I knew it needed a major change in direction. The question was how? I came across a nationally recognized marketing firm, and had the company vetted by friends who knew of them and what they could accomplish. Unfortunately, the marketing firm did not provide what was needed, as they over-promised and under-delivered the national exposure they had promised for my company.

During the process of working with this marketing firm I decided to move to Tampa, Florida to restart my business. This was a perfect fit for the re-organization of my company. Florida has a well-established policy helping small companies to grow without the extreme taxation and anti-business regulations of California. Florida made for a perfect fit!

After I moved to Florida, it became apparent the marketing firm I signed up with did not meet the requirements I expected, and I realized the firm was unethical and duplicitous in its business dealings. As one learns in the military, some things do not turn out the way you want, so you have to adapt and adjust to the changing environment and just keep pushing forward. While in Tampa, I met and joined another marketing firm which provided me with the tools necessary to re-establish my business. As I was changing marketing companies, I decided to rename my company and establish it as Ubaldi Reports. I would write the content on national and international topics, and as it expanded I would bring veterans of the armed forces with expertise on domestic and global issues into my staff of writers.

Ubaldi Reports is a company which provides political content on domestic and global issues, allowing readers access to important, unbiased news and information—a much needed alternative to the mainstream media. A key component would be that I wanted all staff writers to be veterans of the U.S. armed forces.

Into the Fabric of America

During this time, I decided to set up Vet Transition Academy to help provide veterans with the tools necessary to integrate back into the U.S. economy, hoping to help them minimize the problems which I encountered. The purpose was to make sure veterans did not have to go through the same situations I did as they entered the workforce or set up their business. It saddened me to see so many veterans unemployed in a society which doesn't understand their value or how to maximize what they can contribute.

Too often veterans have a higher unemployment rate than non-veterans. The Iraq and Afghanistan Veterans of America reported in a post by research staff member Jaqueline Mafuchi, "Today, the Bureau of Labor Statistics reported that the July 2014 unemployment rate for post-9/11 veterans increased to 9.2%, up from 7.0% in June 2014.

"All veteran unemployment also showed an increase up to 6% from 5.4% in June 2014. The national unemployment rate also increased slightly to 6.2% from 6.1% in June.

"This is the second month in a row that the veteran unemployment rates have increased. While it's still too soon to sound the alarms, overall the veteran and national unemployment rates have been steadily trending downward for months. These numbers remind us that we can't become complacent when it comes to employing our vets. It's in the nation's best interest to ensure that we invest in the future by employing our veterans." (Maffucci 2014)

The Department of Defense will be making substantial reductions in the operating forces in the coming years, thus forcing thousands of veterans to enter the civilian sector and its depressed economy.

On March 5, 2014, the General Accountability Office (GAO) issued a report titled, "Improved Oversight Needed to Enhance Implementation of Transition Assistant Programs." With the draw down from the wars in Iraq and Afghanistan and as the military makes on-going and planned force reductions, many service members are projected to depart the military through 2017. The Transition Assistant Program (TAP) is one of a number of federal programs to assist transitioning service members and veterans in developing job skills and securing civilian employment. TAP serves as a gateway to additional information and services available either while service members are on active duty or after they've separated from the military. (GAO 2014)

Governmental Stumble

The question I would like to ask concerns what many veterans have asked me, "Do Transition Assistance Programs really help transitioning veterans re-enter the private sector and do they provide any useful guidance when starting a business?

For example, the Department of Labor employment workshop highlights many of the skills and techniques helpful in obtaining employment. After completing the workshop, service members can benefit further by returning to the TAP offices where they can access websites intended to introduce participants during TAP training to potential employers. They can also use services at local VA and Department of Labor offices. The GAO also mentions in its report that once veterans depart active service other programs offer services to integrate them into the fabric of US society. Five employment and training programs overseen by the Department of Labor and the Department of Veterans Affairs also help transitioning veterans. (GAO 2014)

But the questions that need to be answered are these: How effective are these programs? Are they beneficial in helping transitioning veterans?

In the President's fiscal year 2015 Veterans Affairs budget, $1 billion has been allocated, over 5 years, for a new veterans' job corps. There will be $106 million to help separating service members transition back into civilian life. (VA 2014)

How are we, as a nation, putting veterans to work? Are we doing so in an effective and concise manner or are we creating programs that are ineffective and unproductive? Let's create a new beginning and truly maximize the innovation and transformation veterans can bring to the U.S. economy.

INTRODUCTION

The conflict in Iraq has ended; soon the conflict in Afghanistan will fade into history as the last U.S. forces pull out by the end of 2016. America now faces a sharp reduction in the Department of Defense and with it hundreds of thousands of veterans will be returning to civilian life. With the economy in a stagnant, depressed state how many of these returning veterans will be able to find meaningful employment for themselves and be able to take care of their families?

The purpose of this book is to convey the veterans' story—those who fought in Iraq and Afghanistan, and to make America aware of the tremendous pool of talent veterans represent and how their skills can be used to rebuild America and not be wasted!

Beginning with the end of the draft in 1973, America has had an all-volunteer military force for forty years. Consequently, today's Americans have little connection to those who serve in the armed forces—those who protect the freedoms we enjoy. Too often we don't have an understanding of what members of the armed forces do, the skills veterans have, and how veterans can transform the American economy and most importantly, transform the American political system.

This book was written to highlight how veterans can revolutionize this country. I want the American people to know—and most importantly—the business community to understand, what an *untapped resource* veterans represent.

My own experience includes two tours of duty in Afghanistan and one tour in Iraq. When I returned home, I felt I had entered a different world. More and more Americans had little or no understanding of my service, with many having never even met anyone who had served in Iraq or Afghanistan. When seeking employment, I found many companies were seeing me through the stereotypical eyes of the media. A lot of businesses wouldn't even consider hiring me because I was a reservist. They thought I would be activated at some point and did not want to take a chance on me. Then there are those employers who assume all veterans have one type of mental health issue or another. The businesses community as a whole has never fully recognized just how much value veterans can add to their companies nor how veterans can and will transform this country— because, perhaps, many business owners themselves have never served.

The U.S. needs to understand—and this book will articulate this—how veterans can impact a business; how veterans will revolutionize this country; and finally, how veterans can utilize their innovative skills for the benefit of American business and the United States. The veterans of World War II transformed the American landscape and had a profound impact on the US economy for decades. Today the veterans of the conflicts in Iraq and Afghanistan can bring about innovative improvements to this country and usher in a revolution in transformational thinking.

In this book I will discuss how a company can benefit from hiring a U.S. military veteran. This book lets veterans know the value they bring to business and most importantly to America.

I will also explain why the country and businesses should invest in a veteran and why businesses should hire a veteran.

I will show how the innovative skills veterans have learned and employed in battle can be efficaciously applied in business. There's a societal misunderstanding of veterans which needs to be addressed and this book will address it! I also delve into how veterans returned from past American conflicts, how they reentered society, and how society accepted them.

Too often there's an under-utilization of veterans—veteran talent which is being wasted because of indifference and lack of knowledge about the valuable capabilities of those who serve in the armed forces of this country.

There are many challenges facing veterans which need to be addressed and which society needs to understand. This book will look into the challenges facing those reserve and National Guard forces who answered the call of duty and left their careers and families behind to preserve our freedoms.

Finally, how do we as a nation integrate veterans back into American society?

This book highlights each of these areas letting the American public know the value veterans bring and how they can impact our economy and our country. This book was written for veterans who answered the call of duty after 9/11 and went off to defend the freedoms we cherish. This nation owes an immeasurable amount of gratitude to all veterans for the sacrifices they have made for our freedom. Veterans gave all they had!

For over thirty years I have had the honor and privilege of serving with some of the finest men and women this country has ever produced. I want America to understand the outstanding quality of the men and women serving in today's armed forces. Americans should be extremely proud of the members of our Armed Forces.

SECTION ONE:
COMING HOME

Each war has its challenges for returning veterans and the veterans returning from Iraq and Afghanistan are no different. The greatest example which is applicable to this generation would be veterans returning from the Second World War. During that period, America had close to 16 million veterans who had served in various capacities. With the war over and millions of veterans returning home, Americans remembered the Great Depression and were fearful veterans would be unable to find work. What was going to happen? Was the nation going to experience another depression because there was not enough viable work for everybody who needed a job?

Workforce.com published an article in their February 26, 2012 edition titled "Fighting for Employment: Veterans in the 1940s and Today." World War II veterans returned home to financial uncertainty. Economic anxiety was the result of the not-so-distant memories of the Great Depression. Today's veterans face not a memory of a depression, but a grim reality of America's current economic plight. America is in decline on all fronts—unrepayable national debt, a stagnant economy where most of the new jobs being created are low paying service sector jobs, diminished manufacturing capability which outsources jobs overseas, a dysfunctional school system, ballooning welfare and social entitlement programs, a government-orchestrated weakening of our military power in the face of growing threats from abroad (Russia and China), and a government which has lost the confidence of its apathetic citizens. In both the 40s and today, the issue of military personnel returning from service created challenges for employers, policy-makers, and the soldiers themselves.

Assimilating veterans back into society has always been a challenge. Over the past several decades, members of the armed forces have returned from a variety of wars and conflicts: World War II, the Korean conflict, the war in Vietnam, the Gulf War in Iraq, and the conflict in Afghanistan. Along the way, they have faced different political, social, and economic situations, including how society views veterans, the benefits bestowed upon them, the type of work available, and the state of the economy. (Greengard 2014)

The Return of the Jedi

"Each generation of veterans is defined by the era in which they served," says Glenn Altschuler, Litwin Professor of American Studies at Cornell University and co-author of The GI Bill: A New Deal for Veterans. However, no period had a greater influence on the military and society than World War II. "The 15.7 million veterans who returned had an undeniable impact on the American economy as well as attitudes about how to assimilate veterans returning from deployment."

After WWII, when the veterans returned home there was a little anxiety, but this was somewhat alleviated by the introduction of the G.I Bill. On June 22, 1944, President Franklin Delano Roosevelt signed the Serviceman's Re-adjustment Act, better known today as the G.I. Bill. The Veterans Administration, as it was known, was charged with carrying out the law's key provisions. (Greengard 2014)

This one act dramatically changed the educational landscape of the United States by paying for college educations for millions of veterans. Prior to WWII, only those who could afford to go to college or had the ability to work their way through school could attend. One only has to understand that before the war started the percentage of Americans in college was extremely low, the country was in a depression and college was out of reach for most Americans and only the wealthy were able to take advantage of higher education. The GI Bill was a phenomenal success by any measure and this one piece of legislation fundamentally transformed America for decades to come, and ushered in the economic boom of the post-World War II era.

As Workforce.com reported, more than half of all soldiers tapped the education benefit in one form or another. In fact, three years after it passed, vets consisted of 49% of all college admissions. These students quickly gained a reputation for their unwavering commitment to learning. The GI Bill helped elevate the US and provide the foundation for today's knowledge-based economy and it also provided vocational and technical training that was greatly needed at the time. (Greengard 2014)

The GI Bill phenomenally changed the US economy. Prior to the GI Bill very few Americans could afford the cost of a college education or move beyond a high school education. Now the opportunity opened up for millions of returning veterans to reach beyond anything they ever dreamed before. Those who chose to go to college had the chance because the government paid them to go. Those who wanted to go through a trade school or an apprenticeship program were also supported by the government. The other aspect of the GI Bill signed by President Roosevelt went beyond just providing educational benefits to returning veterans, but it also gave veterans the ability to receive home, farm, and business loans provided by the federal government. This singular act transformed the American economic system and unleashed a decade of economic growth which otherwise the nation would not have experienced.

Workforce.com reported that a Gallup poll in July, 1944, found that almost 50% of Americans anticipated that the number of unemployed people would range between 7 million and 20 million after the war. At the time, the numbers corresponded to between 14–34% of the civilian workforce. At the same time, the US Labor Department projected an unemployment rate of about 25%. Indeed, in the April, 1945 issue of *Personal Journal* (*Workforce Management's* forbearer), Charles Farmer wrote that 55 to 60 million jobs must be provided if we are to have full employment after the war. Consequently, some organizations (the American Legion was one) opposed the outright demobilization of those in the service without a proper job awaiting them upon their discharge. (Greengard 2014)

The Warrior and America

No one could imagine or foresee the change in the American economy. People were tired of scrimping from the Great Depression and saving during the war years. Now was the time to make up for lost time. Veterans made up for the years missed because of the war, wasted no time, and went to school or sought out other opportunities as they unleashed a juggernaut of economic expansion which has not been seen since.

While visiting the armed forces museum at Largo, Florida, I spoke to one of the docents volunteering there. We were talking about the returning veterans of today, compared to the veterans returning from World War II. The major difference was that in World War II everybody in America served in some capacity, and when the veterans returned, the majority went on to some form of educational pursuit. Statistics from the time have shown that 49% of all college admissions were veterans. (VA 2014) The difference between the two conflicts is that everyone in America served, unlike today's conflicts in Iraq and Afghanistan.

The whole country was mobilized behind the war effort. Korea was like a WWII light. There was still a draft. Then came Vietnam, and with it a change in the social consciousness of the nation. For the first time the nation as a whole did not share in the sacrifice of a conflict, only those drafted or who volunteered served in Vietnam. Many received educational draft deferments if they remained in college. The difference with Vietnam compared with the WWII and Korea generation is only those who didn't go to college went to Vietnam. If you had a college deferment, you didn't have to go to war, you didn't have to join the military, and you didn't have to go through the draft process. The GI bill started to change a little bit, and finally in 1976 the GI bill was abolished and transitioned to a less expansive educational support program provided by the government.

In 1976 the GI Bill was scrapped and transitioned into VEAP (Vocational Education Assistance Program). This new program helped pay my way through junior college, but ended as it only paid a certain amount. After it was exhausted I had to pay the rest of my junior and senior year of college. It was a stark contrast to the GI bill of World War II, as there was no GI Bill until late 1986 when President Ronald Reagan signed into law the new military GI Bill. The new revamped GI Bill signed by President George W. Bush in 2008, modeled after the GI Bill of World War II elevated education so veterans going back to school had their tuition fully funded by the federal government. The new G.I. Bill also included as one of its many provisions a housing stipend to assist the veterans in establishing themselves in college without the additional burden of having to pay for living expenses. Later there was an extension added to the new G.I. Bill in which additional benefits could be extended to a veteran's spouse and children

The Rejected Warrior

The major difference with today's veterans, unlike those after World War II, is that they are enrolling in universities which are totally against the wars in Iraq and Afghanistan.

In 1973, the US government abolished the draft and went to an all-volunteer force. The difference between the Vietnam veterans and the WWII generation was that the Vietnam veterans were abandoned by the country they served; many in society blamed them for the conflict and the social issues that ravaged the country during this turbulent period.

No one really wanted to socialize with veterans from Vietnam, as many blamed soldiers for the problems the nation was experiencing. These veterans entered college and universities, and were treated despicably and negatively by admissions officials, and by college professors as well. Many veterans didn't want to let anybody know they had served in the armed forces.

This situation eerily reminded me of an event when I was young and the Vietnam War was coming to a close. My father knew a family who had two sons, both serving in the Navy. One of the sons served on the aircraft carrier Coral Sea which at the time was home ported at the Alameda Naval Station. This son would visit from time to time and each time my father would ask him to wear his uniform; each time he refused, but finally he relented. When they went out the son had a look of extreme embarrassment on his face, like he was ashamed to be wearing the uniform of the Armed Forces of the United States of America. This was also a reflection of how America looked at its sons and daughters in uniform.

The Return

I've talked to many veterans who are in their early twenties and are going back to college or entering college for the first time and feel alienated from many of their peers. They are facing instructors hostile to the very fact they served in Iraq or Afghanistan. What do they get—alienation! They don't have anybody they can relate to, as most of their colleagues or fellow students have never served in the military or don't know what they were going through. You have college professors or academics looking at them with disdain because of their service.

On Military.com, army veteran Ben Miller remembers the isolation he felt when he enrolled in the University of Missouri/ St. Louis. "I would show up on campus, talk to absolutely no one and go home," said Miller, 27, who did three tours in Iraq as a counter-intelligence specialist. "I didn't feel like I really belonged." This is coming out of the St. Louis Post Dispatch.

Some academics and veteran advocates are warning that many colleges are unprepared to deal with the unique needs of former service members. Many veterans face a difficult transition to civilian life ranging from adjustment issues to recovery from physical and mental issues. (Military.com)

The key component of this is you go to college, or a university, and your fellow students have no clue what it was like or what or what you did in the military. They may support you in what you did, but it's always tempered with, "I support you, but I don't agree with us being in Iraq and Afghanistan." How does that make a veteran feel if they say 'we support you but we don't support your mission'? The Vietnam veteran and the War on Terror veteran of Iraq and Afghanistan have something that unites them. We were not treated the way the Vietnam veteran was treated by society at large. This was thanks to all Vietnam veterans who made sure what happened to them would not happen to us! Every chance I get I thank Vietnam veterans for making sure my life was easier than what they faced. I can never thank them enough!

The similarities are the same. People aren't openly critical of us, but at the same time we're going into a workforce where people don't understand what we do. The general public is isolated from the wars in Iraq and Afghanistan. I've met very few individuals who have served in Iraq or Afghanistan. You go into the workforce and you have employers who don't know what you do. The only thing they have is what they view on television or what they see in the media. This is what veterans face. This is where the similarities with the Vietnam vets come in.

The Wolf, the Sheep, and the Sheepdog

There is a book titled, *On Combat: The Psychology and Physiology of Deadly Combat in War and Peace* written by Lieutenant Colonel Dave Grossman with Lauren W. Christiansen. Beginning on page 182 he divides people into three groups, "the sheep", "the wolves", and "the sheepdogs". He writes, "Let me expand on this old soldier's excellent model of sheep, wolves, and sheepdogs. We know that the sheep live in denial. That is what makes them sheep. They do not want to believe that there's evil in the world. They can accept the fact that fires can happen which is why they want fire extinguishers, fire sprinklers, fire alarms, and fire exits throughout their kids' schools. But many of them are outraged at the idea of putting an armed police officer in their kids' school. Our children are dozens of times more likely to be killed and thousands of times more likely to be seriously injured by school violence than by school fires.

"The sheep's only response to the possibility of violence is denial. The idea of someone coming to kill or harm their children is just too hard, so they choose the path of denial. The sheep generally do not like the sheepdog. He looks a lot like the wolf; he has fangs and the capacity for violence. The difference though is that the sheepdog must not, cannot, and will not ever harm the sheep. Any sheep dog that intentionally harms the lowliest little lamb will be punished and removed. The world can't work any other way, at least, not in a representative democracy or republic such as ours.

"Still this sheepdog disturbs the sheep. He is the constant reminder that there are wolves in the land. They would prefer that he didn't tell them where to go or give them traffic tickets or stand at the ready in our airports in camouflaged fatigues holding an M-16. The sheep would rather have the sheepdog cash in his fangs, spray paint himself white and go, 'Baaah!' Until the wolf shows up! Then the entire flock tries desperately to hide behind one lowly sheepdog.

"As Kipling said in his poem about Tommy, the British soldier, "While it's Tommy this and Tommy that and Tommy fall behind, but it's please to walk in front, sir, when there's trouble in the wind. There's trouble in the wind, my boys. There's trouble in the wind. Oh, it's please to walk in front, sir, when there's trouble in the wind.

"Understand there is nothing morally superior about being a sheepdog. It is just what you chose to be. Also understand that a sheepdog is a funny critter. He's always sniffing around out on the perimeter—checking the breeze, barking at things that go bump in the night, and yearning for a righteous battle. That is, the young sheepdogs yearn for a righteous battle. The old sheepdogs are a little older and wiser, but they move to the sound of the guns when needed right along with the young ones. Here is how the sheep and sheepdog think differently. The sheep pretend the wolf will never come, but the sheepdog lives for that day. After the attacks of September 11, 2001, most of the sheep—that is, most citizens in America—said, 'Thank God I wasn't on one of those planes.' The sheepdogs, the warriors, said, 'Dear God, I wish I could have been one of those planes. Maybe I could have made a difference.' When you are truly transformed into a warrior and have truly invested yourself into a warrior herd you want to be there. You want to be able to make a difference.

"Some people may be designed to be sheep, and others may be genetically primed to be wolves or sheepdogs. But I believe that most people choose which one they want to be, and I'm proud to say that more and more Americans are choosing to be sheep-dogs." (Grossman 2004)

Here's the point the author is trying to make and the point I'd like to emphasize, especially to the thousands of police officers and soldiers I speak to each year. This goes also to the citizens of this country who are not veterans who've served their country.

"In nature, the real sheep are born as sheep. Sheepdogs are born that way and so are wolves. They didn't have a choice, but you do, and you are not a critter. As a human being, you can be what-ever you want to be. It is a conscious moral decision. If you want to be a sheep, then you can be a sheep and that is okay. But you must understand the price you pay. When the wolf comes, you and your loved ones are going to die if there's no sheepdog there to protect you. If you want to be a wolf, you can be one, but the sheepdogs are going to hunt you down and you will never have rest, safety, trust, or love. If you want to be a sheepdog and follow the warrior's path then you must make a conscious and moral decision every day to dedicate, equip, and prepare yourself to prevail in that moment when the wolf appears at the door." (Grossman 2004)

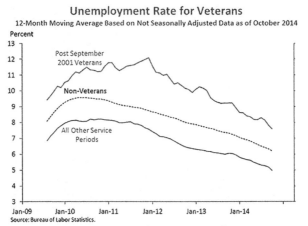

Figure 1: US News: Unemployment Rate for Veterans 2014

In this analogy between the wolf, the sheepdog, and the sheep, veterans are the sheepdogs. They protect this country against those who would do us harm. They sit on the wall standing watch while others lie snug in their homes. It's the sheepdog that protects this country. It's always been the sheepdog that protects this country. But as the sheepdog gets old, as the sheepdog retires, as the sheepdog melds back into society, that sheepdog should be honored and not reviled.

The sheepdog should be able to go to college and not be looked upon as something to ridicule or disdain because he chose the life of a warrior to protect this country as the sheepdog protects the flock. The veteran protects this nation. The veteran should be able to come back and not be looked at as he or she has PTSD or all the problems associated with it. The veteran should be taken care of and should have an honored place in society, much like the Spartan warriors of ancient Greece.

SECTION TWO:
A HERO RETURNS

First Lady Michelle Obama, speaking at the Veterans Full Employment Act of 2013 Bill signing ceremony stated, "With the Iraq war over, the war in Afghanistan winding down, more than a million service members are going to be hanging up their uniforms and transitioning back to civilian life. That comes on top of the hundreds of thousands of veterans and military spouses already out there and looking for work."

The First Lady continued, "So even though we've made a lot of progress on veterans' employment over the past few years, as a country, we still have a lot more work to do. That means we need to redouble our efforts across the board. We need more businesses to make big, bold commitments to hire and train our veterans and military spouses. We need more hospitals and colleges and employers from every sector to recognize our veterans' and military spouses' unique skills and experiences and give them a fair shot at a job. We need every single state that has not already acted on those licensing and credentialing issues to follow Maryland's lead and clear away every unnecessary obstacle facing our veterans and military spouses." (Obama 2013)

We Don't Hire Your Kind

The question which needs to be asked is this: Why aren't businesses hiring veterans?

Fortune magazine on November 11, 2013, carried the article: "Three Reasons Why Companies Do Not Hire Veterans".

First are the assumptions and stereotypes about members of the military that make some employers reluctant to hire them. About one in three employers consider Post Traumatic Stress Disorder to be an impediment to hiring a veteran, according to a survey report by the Society for Human Resource Management. (Reynolds Lewis 2013)

I personally had to answer this question on a radio show when I was interviewed. Before the Fourth of July weekend in 2014, a radio station was doing a story on fireworks and PTSD (Post Traumatic Stress Disorder). This topic had been floating around the Internet and many news affiliates were covering this story to see if there was any correlation between fireworks and veterans as it potentially makes them relive their war experiences.

The radio station wanted to know what it is like when fireworks go off, and would they be a triggering problem for veterans. Would the exploding of fireworks cause veterans to relive the trauma and chaos experienced in Iraq and Afghanistan. My response was that each veteran is different, but far too often we erroneously consider PTSD as a universal condition among veterans, thinking all veterans have this mental disorder. This is far from the truth, but some believe it applies to all veterans.

How can you blame the general public, as any time they watch a television program there seems to be a commercial about wounded or mental health issues among veterans? If this is all they see, how can you blame businessmen who would be reluctant to hire veterans because of PTSD related issues? Many groups run commercial ads highlighting the need to assist veterans who have combat related physical or mental injuries. These organizations do good work, but they perpetrate a stereotype that all veterans are injured in some capacity.

This is why I make a conscious decision not to watch certain television programs. Many of them misleadingly and negatively stereotype all veterans as having mental health problems.

It is so sad that the general public sees veterans constantly portrayed in the news and entertainment media as suffering from mental health issues. It's no wonder some businesses are reluctant to hire veterans. When I was attending my transition assistance program while on active duty, one of the Marines attending with me mentioned he was asked in an employment interview, "Do I need to worry about you coming in here and shooting up the place?" To me this is not only regrettable, but more importantly, this is a disturbing statement to make to a veteran who served his country.

Falling through the Cracks

In the second part of the *Fortune* magazine article, which also discusses why veterans are not hired, I described the many vaguely defined or misunderstood skills which employers do not understand. Employers can easily understand a resume showing a college degree in a related field and one entry-level job. It's not so clear what an Ordinance Specialist or Petty Officer can offer a civilian employer. (Reynolds Lewis 2013)

One retired Marine included his rank and the fact that he was a mid-level to senior level manager on his resume. The company he was applying to did not understand the rank structure or believe him regarding his skills or experience. Their response was that there was no way he could do what he claimed. They just did not understand the military places a greater degree of responsibility in its personnel which is not the case in the private sector. The other problem was that there was not sufficient commonality between the veteran and the employer. The employer had no idea what caliber of an individual was there in the interview, because he had no association with anyone who served in the armed forces.

Since so many in the business community have never served, they have no idea what a veteran can do or how to benefit from the veteran's experience. Businesses and human resource departments have no detailed, realistic view of what life is like in the military. Human resource software looks for key words or phrases that do not show up in military skill sets no matter how appropriate they may be.

Even when applying for government employment, veterans face the same problem. This affected a government position I was applying for. The head of the department told me I met all the requirements, but I would have to go through the USAJobs online employment center. I met every requirement listed in the job announcement; I made it through the first round of scrutiny, but eventually was denied the position. The department head said they were looking for various key words, but none of the key words the department was looking for, or the experience I had, was listed in the announcement. I had the skills and the experience needed, but because of the way resumes are processed I was denied a position.

How many veterans cannot communicate their value because of human resource software? Corporate America is failing to recognize the potential benefits of hiring veterans because they fail to maintain comprehensive databases that contain military duty terminology.

Skills Transfer

Skill sets gained in the military can be maximized and transferred by ensuring that skills, training, and certifications have a dual purpose—both military and civilian. Too often the skills and training obtained in the military cannot be transferred to the civilian sector. Not all veterans are going to go to college. Maybe not all veterans want to go to college, but some of the skills they have serve dual purposes. I know one former Marine who was a motor transport operator. She can drive any large vehicle in the military arsenal, but yet as soon as she transitioned into the private sector she found her certifications were not transferable. She can't even drive a cab, but yet she can drive anything the military has, and can do it in a combat environment. What a waste of talent, and for that matter, what a waste of all the training and money the government spent!

When she transitioned out of the military, the government had to spend thousands of additional dollars to re-train her in a field where she was already more than amply qualified to perform. Why couldn't they transfer those same skills to give her a viable job and a viable opportunity when she transitioned to the civilian economy. This is an example of ignoring available resources, another expensive bureaucratic mistake!

The same goes for medical personnel in the armed forces. We have many medical personal performing incredible things in Iraq and Afghanistan—handling triage cases, handling multiple combat injuries, yet when they transition to the private sector, they can't even get a job as an ambulance driver because they're not certified in the private sector. What a waste of an expensive resource, and most importantly the waste of taxpayer money, especially in these times of widespread government financial distress (bankruptcy). It's definitely not a smart business move!

President Obama stated in 2012, "Let me tell you something, if you can save a life on the battlefield, you can save a life in an ambulance. If you can oversee a convoy of millions of dollars of assets in Iraq, you can help manage a supply chain or balance the books here at home." The President also said, "If you can maintain the most advanced weapons in the world, if you're an electrician on a Navy ship, well, you can manufacture the next generation of advanced technology in our factories," like the factory where he spoke. "If you're working on complex machinery, you should be able to take those skills and find a manufacturing job right here—right here at home." (Obama 2012)

But unfortunately, as the president stated, many returning veterans with such advanced skills don't get hired simply because they don't have the civilian licenses or certifications a lot of companies are required by law to have. That's a mistake! That's not utilizing or maximizing veterans who are trained and equipped to handle these positions in the private sector. From an economic standpoint this is a total waste of taxpayer money. Right now, legislation is slowly winding its way through Congress looking to rectify this situation. It ensures that certifications gained in the military can be transferred to the private sector.

Businesses Lack of Faith

Finally, the last part many employers worry about when hiring veterans is that they may end up being short-staffed if the military reverses course and calls up former service members. This is a question many businesses ask themselves. Is this veteran going to be yanked from under me and sent overseas? This is the question heard by Dan Goldenberg, Executive Director of the Call of Duty Endowment, a non-profit organization that recognizes and funds organizations that put veterans into great jobs. If a veteran is in active reserves status, he is supposed to inform his employer (Reynolds-Lewis 2013)

If you inform a prospective employer that you are a reservist you may not be offered a position, but if you do not, an employer could terminate you for providing false information. It's like you are damned if you do and damned if you don't.

This is a situation I personally faced after all of my three deployments—first in Afghanistan, then in Iraq, and finally my last deployment again to Afghanistan. In 2007, I left a consulting firm to find employment elsewhere. Each time, being a veteran, or more specifically being on active reserve was a red flag on my resume. Employers always asked, "Are going to deploy?" Granted they're not supposed to ask that question, but then the veteran has to prove they asked the question, and they intentionally discriminated against the veteran because he was a veteran and a military reservist.

How many businesses have been fined by the U.S. Justice Department for unfavorable hiring practices as it relates to veterans and military reservists? If there are any, I'd like to know their names.

This discrimination makes finding employment a little bit harder and a little bit more frustrating. Even though the wars in Iraq and Afghanistan are winding down, most employers are still looking at the fact that a veteran is an active reservist, and could be called to active duty if the military decides to reverse course. If you look around the world today, you see trouble brewing in many regions which could call for the deployment of military personnel, and would include military reservists and National Guard personnel. This is what makes it harder for a lot of reservists to find employment.

Government Tries to Intervene

On September 11, 2013, the *National Journal* wrote, "In 2011, President Obama challenged the private sector to hire and train 100,000 veterans and military spouses by the end of 2013. Since that time dozens of employers have made vocal commitments to do so. Last August, First Lady Michelle Obama announced that these efforts had already led to 125,000 hires. At the same time, corporate commitments to hire veterans and reintegrate them into the civilian workforce have forced many companies to take a hard look at their hiring practices." The *National Journal* continued, "Former service members have become a minority population little understood by many civilians." (Quinton 2013)

Has anyone followed up to see if this challenge by the president has been fulfilled?

As the president challenged the private sector to hire veterans, how many business leaders know anything about the military or have been on a military installation? This is an issue I faced first hand, as most Americans live far from any military base. In March of 2014 I retired from the Marines, and my brother made a startling statement when he came to my retirement banquet at Camp Pendleton. This was the first time he had been on a military base since he was in high school. He's in his forties now; it has been well over 25 years since he's been on a military base. How many other Americans, including our business leaders, have the same experience of having never been on military base? Currently less than 1% of the US population has served on active duty in the last decade.

"On the private sector side, there's a lack of understanding of the breadth of occupations and the jobs that people hold in the military," says James Schmelling, managing director and co-founder of the Institute for Veterans and Military Families at Syracuse University. "Many military jobs involve responsibilities that aren't reflected in their official title like 'logistics' or 'project management'. This is also a difficult issue for veterans to address themselves as many veterans are unsure how to translate their military skills and experience into civilian skills needed by or sought after by employers." (Quinton 2013)

The *National Journal* continued, "Corporate commitments provide a bridge from the military to the civilian labor market, but they can't address labor market challenges that all job-seekers face. Businesses are missing an excellent opportunity to hire innovative employees residing in the armed forces of the United States

"We know that a major barrier to entry, especially in this economy, is not having the educational experience a company is looking for," says Bryan Hawthorn, an Iraq war veteran and board member for Student Veterans of America. "Veterans with advanced degrees are much more likely to find employment and to find family supporting jobs than those with just a high school diploma. Likewise, those who go home to poor or rural areas (where jobs are scarce) struggle to find work just like their neighbors do." (Quinton 2013)

Figure 2: MGySgt John Ubaldi

Vocational skills and the programs set up by the Department of Veterans Affairs and the Department of Labor need to be audited to find out if they are serving the needs of their target market. Far too often millions are spent by various agencies to integrate veterans back into the society, but like all federal programs the programs are not analyzed and audited to verify they are meeting their objectives.

What are the measures of performance and effectiveness of these programs? Typically we spend millions upon millions of dollars but seldom check to see if any of these programs are successful in training veterans for vocational employment and placing them into viable jobs so they can provide for their families. We know of programs like "Helmets to Hardhats," but how effective are they?

Who oversees many of the state and local veteran integration programs? Various states have instituted their own programs, but how effective are they?

Where Have All the Leaders Gone?

Forbes magazine published another article in its October 12, 2013 edition titled, "Why a Veteran Might Be Your Next Best Hire." This was written by Shane Robinson who himself was an active duty soldier in the US Army. As he was writing this article, he stated as an entrepreneur, "Therefore, I feel a sense of responsibility to be part of the solution. I think now, perhaps more than ever, start-ups are in a position to grow their ranks and simultaneously reduce veteran unemployment and to prove that it is an accomplishable mission for companies—up-starts and established alike. I enlisted the help of LinkedIn, ID.me and Calloway Capital Management to understand the reasons why these trendsetting start-ups hired veterans." (Robinson 2013)

In his article he discussed a couple of different topics. The first was leadership readiness at every level. Working in an entrepreneurial environment is like working in professional sports or rock n' roll. What matters most is not your age or tenure but rather the quality of your contribution. Often you must be prepared to inherit a leadership role at a young age. Many veterans were placed in charge of millions of dollars' worth of classified equipment. I know of colleagues who in their 20s were appointed interim governors of entire towns in the Middle East. So it was no surprise when LinkedIn said the following about one of their veterans, "Ben Fa, who along with fellow intern, Tom Pei, spearheaded an initiative during "In Day" to give over 100 vet's free LinkedIn profile makeovers." (Robinson 2013)

I had experienced some of these things that Mr. Robinson talked about in his article. As a Civil Affairs Marine in Afghanistan and Iraq, I viewed first hand young Marines—19, 20, 21 years-old—in charge of towns, handling millions of US reconstruction dollars to provide construction contracts, with oversight and project management responsibilities for constructing buildings and roads. They were in charge of millions of dollars of sophisticated equipment and doing things their contemporaries back home with no military experience could only dream about doing. These skills could not just be used in an entrepreneurial manner, but could be applied in any business. They have the training; they have the skills. They just need the opportunity to be involved!

Combat Proven Leader

Robinson continued, "The next phase is composure and creativity under pressure. Working in a start-up equates to operating under extreme pressure. Despite the rigidity of military regulations and the certainty provided by standard operating procedures, officers and enlisted soldiers alike are accustomed to making significant decisions in the face of moral dilemmas, the threat of physical harm, and a myriad of complex, time-critical situations. The ability to creatively solve problems in the face of unprecedented situations is a quality for which the start-up ID.me has found immensely valuable." (Robinson 2013)

In my service in Iraq and Afghanistan, I saw this time and time again. Many times we had to make snap decisions under pressure—under combat, under fire, under situations where we suffered from lack of sleep, conditions that most civilians would find appalling. Even if you're working on base, computers go down on a routine basis because of the conditions of the heat and elements, but you still have to get your job done. You can't go to your commander and say, "Well, I'm sorry, sir. The computer crashed; I can't do my job." That's not going to happen. You still have to conduct your job even in the most adverse situations.

The other thing that Mr. Robinson mentioned was the big-picture understanding and relentless attention to detail. The minimum viable product within the start-up culture is based on the notion of providing just enough detail to serve the higher strategy. The military phrase, "Good enough for government work" is actually a suitable comparison here. In all seriousness, vets are trained to keep a watchful eye on the big picture while maintaining an absolute understanding of detail. Such ability is incredibly rare and particularly important to the emerging market investment company, Calloway Capital Management. This company was quick to point to Scott Quigley (yet another veteran intern) as an example of one who possesses this talent. (Robinson 2013)

All veterans have a big picture mentality. One of the key components of military planning is knowing the commander's intent, and knowing the responsibilities of commanders at least two levels above your own, if not higher. It is drilled into all veterans to know the job of the person above them to ensure they can get the job done in case they have to assume responsibility for that position, so as not to compromise the mission. This attention to detail is one of the most important attributes of any veteran, no matter what rank or branch of service they belong to.

All these attributes are highly sought after in the private sector. Businesses just need to leverage and realize these are the qualities a veteran can bring to their company that can help it maintain its profitability and expand its business.

The Band of Brothers

Another thing Robinson mentioned was the ultimate team-player mentality. One of the key leadership tenets we learn in the military is that in order to become a good leader one must first be a good follower. In this sense, rising through the ranks is a rite of passage that allows all military leaders to develop their own management styles based on the observation of their superiors, both good and bad along the way. Working in a dynamic corporation requires a similar maturation through the accumulation process. Often the most effective leaders are those who are able to mobilize their teams from the bottom of the chain of command simply by setting the right example for others to follow. (Robinson 2013)

Robinson also recommended developing management styles based on the observation of superiors, both good and bad. I had many good officers and many officers whose leadership or management styles I would question, but each of them taught me something about becoming a better leader and a better manager. I had one commanding officer, while serving in Afghanistan who always said, "Do things ethically, morally, and legally right and you won't go wrong." You don't have to be the best at everything, but pick the right people and the right positions and train them. Let them do their jobs and give them the guidance they need to accomplish their goal. To be a good leader, one must be a good follower. That skill is something a veteran can bring to any business.

In the military, you have to work with individuals from diverse backgrounds and still be able to accomplish the mission. As a

Marine veteran, I've had to work with people from all ethnic and religious backgrounds. Some come from different parts of the country. Some come from broken homes. Some come from the rural areas—farms, ranches, and the bayous of Louisiana. You have to work together to accomplish the mission. A veteran can be a positive asset for any business and help make it successful.

Integrity-Non-Negotiable

An uncompromising integrity, as Robinson mentioned, is necessary in creating relationships with employees, strategic partners, clients, and investors, and it can single-handedly build or destroy a company. It is also one of the most transferable characteristics veterans bring to the private sector. (Robinson 2013)

As a Marine (and the other branches are no different), integrity is one of the most important traits that you can have. If you can't trust your leader, you'll follow him or her because you have to, but a leader should want you to follow them because you *want* to. You cannot build an organization if its leaders aren't trusted. This is what veterans bring to a business because they understand what integrity is. Our political leaders need to learn this!

Goal orientated veterans are accustomed to not only accessing situations and quickly formulating actionable plans but they are also accustomed to performing after action reviews which require all members of a team to identify areas in which a given strategy could be improved the next time. Start-ups call this process "validating learning." (Robinson 2013)

It's an integral component of the continued forward momentum. Goal orientation or goal orienting is a hallmark of the military. Whatever we do—every exercise, every function we execute, there are always after-action reviews. Everybody has a buy-in, from the top commander to the lowest level Marine, soldier, airman, or sailor. We're always seeking self-improvement—how we can make this action better? A business would love to have employees who want to improve their quality. If you're a customer service oriented business, you're looking for any way to improve that customer service because that's going to make you profitable. A veteran understands this process.

The Risk Taker

Finally, Robinson mentioned that building a start-up, or any organization for that matter, is like starting a revolution. As an entrepreneur, you're convincing anyone you can, your employees, your clients, your partners, and your family that you're engaged in something worth fighting for. It's a grind; it's a battle. So who better to hire than a soldier, sailor, airman or Marine. (Robinson 2013)

This is the one thing all veterans have. They want to make themselves better, and they're always striving to make themselves better. Starting a business involves risk and requires dedication. Who better to have than a veteran who understands what risk is and what goal orientating is? All these things Robinson mentions in his article, all these things are validated. This is what a veteran has! This is what a veteran trains for! This is what a veteran can bring to any organization or business to help it be better organized and more profitable.

Using *Forbes 800* and *Execucomp* surveys that identify company CEOs, and aided by additional research into military service, age, and education, Benmelech and Frydman were able to compare firms run by veterans and those run by executives without any military experience. Then they asked the question: "Has the disappearance of executives who served in the military from the C-suite had a real impact on corporate America?"

The answer, in short, is: Yes.

"Military CEOs seem to cope better under pressure, which is important for firms that experience distress, or for firms that operate in industries that are in distress." The authors told me, "This seems to stem from military training and experience in difficult situations."

In addition, "Military CEOs are also more conservative in making investments and are much less likely to be involved in financial fraud." (Gavett 2014)

Apparently, if there were more veterans on Wall Street and in Washington we may not have had the financial meltdown of 2008-2009, and maybe we would not be faced with the increasingly dysfunctional government in Washington. This evaluation is well-documented and it is also a widely held belief of a large percentage of the American people.

SECTION THREE:
KNOW YOURSELF

Whether you plan to make a career in the military or just complete one enlistment, you should have a plan for your life after your time in the armed forces. Remember this; you have value as a veteran! The training, skills, and experience you received in the armed forces have a direct correlation to what companies—small businesses, larges companies, and governments—desire to enhance their organization, competitiveness, and profitability. As a veteran, you have a special value!

There are two examples I would like to present that will help veterans understand their value! I want to emphasize the value of a military background and how to use it to your advantage in your post-service environment.

Example One. While serving on active duty, as an activated reservist, I would always ask military personnel I was assigned to what they were going to do if their military career ended today. One of them was a senior level sergeant major in a very prominent position—counseling and guiding Marines on what they do in the Marine Corps, but also what they were going to do as they prepared to leave the Marines. This sergeant major was getting ready for retirement (within about a month) and I asked him, "What are you going to do once you retire?" He told me he was going to go to school. Okay, that's pretty good. "So, what are you going to study in school?" I asked. He said he didn't know. Here's a man who spent thirty years in the Marine Corps and really did not know what he wanted to do once he retired from the Marine Corps because he did not know the value he had!

Example Two. I met another Marine at a local barbershop when I was getting my haircut one Saturday. I like to talk to Marines and at least give them my experience because as a reservist with firsthand knowledge I know what life is like outside in the private sector. So I asked this young Marine, "So, what are you going to do? Are you going to stay in? Are you going to get out of the Marine Corps?" He said he was going to get out. I said, "Are you married?"

He said, "Yeah, I'm married and I have two kids."

What do you plan to do? What kind of employment do you plan on seeking when you leave the Marine Corps?" Well, he planned on going back to Texas and getting a position in the oil and gas sector. He had about six months to go. So, I asked him, "Have you set something up?"

He said, "No, I'm just going to wait until I get out and figure it out from then."

I told him, "Don't wait until you get out. Get everything planned now. You have value as a veteran! Plan this beforehand while you still have income as a Marine because as soon as you leave active duty all entitlements stop."

Now, if you have 20 years or more, and you're preparing to retire, the benefits you received on active duty are going to be far different when you transition to civilian life. You may live close to a military base or you may not. You may live well away from a base. It's going to be very different than life in the armed forces.

So, I told this Marine, "Prepare now, keep the money coming in and get a job lined up so when you get out you can seamlessly transition into civilian employment and you don't have a disruption in your income. This is especially important when you have a wife and two children."

Warrior Blueprint for Corporate America

Every veteran has value! They just need to know what their value is. Before you transition out of the military, have a plan! As mandated by the Department of Defense every veteran has to attend TAP classes or a Transition Assistance class. The first step is to know your value. From there you need to figure out what you want to do, where you want to live, and what employment you will be seeking. If you have family, you need to address the relocation of your family to your new home. If you already have it established, you need to ensure the transition proceeds smoothly.

The University of Colorado in Denver, in conjunction with the Denver Chamber of Commerce, listed the top ten reasons why companies would want veterans on their staff (UC Denver & Denver Metro Chamber of Commerce 2014). I will cover each of these points and note where veterans have special values.

1. All companies want leaders. Leadership epitomizes the military. In the military, soldiers are taught to lead from day one. One example, as a young PFC, I was put in charge of a working party and we didn't accomplish our task. I was counseled and I shifted the blame to my Marines, because they didn't do what I told them to do.

   The first thing the leader told me was this: do not blame your men! If we train you to be a leader; you lead! I always remembered his advice. Veterans are trained to lead by example. Veterans understand how to instruct, delegate, motivate, and inspire. Even in the most difficult circumstances, we're always taught to be a leader; whether in peace-time or not. Many of us have served combat tours in Iraq and Afghanistan in some of the most difficult circumstances and we are always trained to lead by example. Make sure your equipment is ready. Make sure your men and the military personnel you're in charge of have their equipment ready and know what to do and what's expected of them. Always leading by example is the most fundamental aspect of the armed forces. This is a value that veterans bring; this is the value which veterans can bring to any employer!

2. Companies like to work with team players. This epitomizes the veteran! This epitomizes the values all veterans hold! United States military veterans understand that individual efforts support the group in reaching a larger objective. They know that a mission can only succeed if everyone on the team is on board. This value characterizes the military culture. The military is always working as a whole. What's best for the unit? Not what is best for the individual! What's best for that individual section, unit, business, company, and battalion? It's working as a team to support a common goal, especially in combat. In combat, you *have to* work as a team! If the unit does not work as a team then the unit cannot be successful, and lives can be in jeopardy.

3. Companies need employees who can perform under pressure. Again this exemplifies and maximizes the value veterans have. This is what you have; you know what it's like to work under pressure. Veterans know how to accomplish their work in the face of limited resources, changing priorities, and often, high levels of stress. They are familiar with high stakes and recognize the importance of staying on task until the work is *done right.*

Veterans *know* this. They know how to perform under pressure. There's nothing greater than the pressure of being in combat. Whether you served in combat or whether you served in a stateside or an overseas location, you're still performing under stress and under a time constraint. You're trying to get the mission accomplished in a timely fashion and often with limited resources. Many times while serving in Iraq or Afghanistan we had limited resources, but we still had to get the job done! There are changing requirements and missions. Most of the time it was under a high level of stress, we still had to get the job done to move forward and accomplish our mission.

4. Companies want well-trained and educated workforces. The military today has changed dramatically from the day I joined back in 1982. When I enlisted, the only ones who had any kind of college experience or education were officers. Today, a good portion of the enlisted ranks have some college. Some have bachelor's degrees, and a few have master's degrees. I knew one sergeant who was working on her PhD in Education. These are values soldiers bring. If you are reading this book and you have a year left or you are just beginning your career in the military, take the time to get involved in the multitude of off-duty education programs (which are often subsidized) to allow you to go to school so you can get your degree or some type of skill or certification you will need when you transfer back to the civilian workforce or the private sector. Veterans have been very well trained to do specific jobs within the military. Their training is complemented by the quality of their education. Companies are willing to hire vets because it saves them training costs. Veterans are very adaptable to training in different careers or in different skills. I had four different military occupational skills and many veterans have similar training. We're adaptable, easy to train, and willing to work hard to succeed in anything we do. This is a valuable trait that can be brought to a business.

5. Companies appreciate employees who understand diversity. Veterans have worked side-by-side with individuals of diverse race, gender, geographic origin, ethnic background, religion and economic status. When you enter the military, you are working with the cross-section of the American landscape. You have to get outside your comfort zone. When you first join the military, you're probably not going to be married. You're going to be put in a room with somebody you don't know. You're not given a choice who your roommate is going to be and you still have to work together to accomplish your assignments. This epitomizes the value that veterans hold.

6. You understand the advantages of seeing the big picture. Companies want to see that their employees understand the strategic concept of the big picture. For example, while I served in the reserves, I worked for USAA, an insurance company catering to the military. Our section had to go to a meeting to discuss a changing strategic concept the company was to begin implementing. You could tell who had military training because they understood the strategic direction the company was going. They saw the big picture! They saw where the company was going strategically. They could think outside of their own myopic unit or section. Those who didn't have military experience weren't able to see the big picture. They saw what they wanted to see or they saw their own little section. Veterans see the big picture, even if they haven't served overseas. Veterans are trained to think globally. They're able to think globally, strategically, tactically, and operationally. They're aware of international trends in business and in industry because they've seen a diverse background. Many veterans have served not only in stateside positions but overseas, so they've seen the way different cultures operate in various countries.

7. You know that work ethic matters. This is the difference between the millennial generation and the generation of today. Veterans understand a work ethic. They're accustomed to working long hours in non-traditional environments. They know what it is to work hard, pay attention to detail, and be resourceful to get the results they need to accomplish the mission. Veterans know that when their commander or section leader comes to them, they're not asking him why they can't get something done. They want to know how they will get the job done. A veteran knows and always has a can-do attitude and is going to be resourceful to get the end results to accomplish the mission that is assigned to him. This is a value that companies want and need, and this is what veterans have!

8. You value procedure and policy in the workforce. Companies are always looking for employees who value procedure and policy in the workplace. Veterans understand their place within an organizational framework. They respect policies and procedures and have learned to be responsible for subordinates and accountable to their managers. Veterans understand a clear-cut chain of command and system. They understand organizational framework. They understand policies and procedures because the military's whole being is about policy and procedures. This is the value that a veteran brings.

9. Another plus that companies will appreciate is that they will save time and money on background checks. Almost all veterans have some type of security clearance, and have gone through some type of background check. They've been through drug testing; they don't have to be tested for drugs. They've gone through this numerous times in their careers. When I first came to the Marine Corps, we were tested twice a week because that was the standard operating procedure. Drug testing is a routine part of a veteran's life in the military. So when companies come in, they're going to save on background checks that are costly and time-consuming. The majority of military members already have some type of clearance and they come with first-hand knowledge of the various government procedures for this.

10. Veterans also develop a strong veteran network. Veterans are connected to other veterans. Veterans like to hire veterans and they meet more quality candidates that can be brought to a company. So veterans have a value that they offer an employer. You just need to know what your value is and redefine what you've learned and what you did in the military and adapt that to the civilian sector and the company you will be working for.

Understanding Global Dynamics

Edward Alden posted an article on the website of the Council on Foreign Relations on January 26, 2012 and said, "Nearly 30% of the US economy is now wrapped up in international trade and half of US growth since the official end of the recession in 2009 has come from exports. The fastest growing economies in the world are not English-speaking. The most promising export sector for the United States is business services which often require face-to-face interactions with foreign customers." The author also stated, "Future US growth will increasingly depend on selling US goods and services to foreign customers who do not necessarily speak English." (Alden 2012)

The global economy has impacted the U.S. economy and veterans have experienced diverse cultures and know how to interact in a global environment. Experienced veterans bring vast resources, innovation, and can help maximize a company's global presence. Businesses today are acting in a global manner, almost all veterans have deployed at some point. Whether they saw combat in Iraq and Afghanistan or throughout the Middle East, most veterans have traveled to Asia, Latin America, Europe, Africa and many diverse places across the globe. Many veterans speak several foreign languages, and have experience with different cultures.

While serving in Iraq, Afghanistan, Asian nations, throughout the Pacific Rim, and in Central America as a member of a Civil Affairs unit, I had to interact with companies operating in foreign countries. I had to deal with military personnel from host countries. I had to deal with civilians from those countries, had to write contracts, make sure contracts were implemented, and had to deal with diverse cultures far different from my own and understand how these dealings would impact the strategic concept of an organization.

You have to understand other cultures and ways of life. As Americans, we may have one set of business values, but not everybody implements business practices like the United States.

While I was in the Civil Affairs unit, the Marines sent elements of my unit to the University of California at Irvine where we took an international negotiation class. As we deployed across the world, we had to learn to negotiate in foreign lands and understand how they saw things. Everyone negotiates at a different level. The Japanese and Chinese negotiate differently, the Americans negotiate differently. Working in a Middle Eastern culture brings a whole different set of ways of conducting business, but at the same time we must maintain our strategic objectives.

Veterans, have to be innovative, adaptable, able to exercise conceptual understanding of the mission, and able to implement the plan. So if you want to be successful, you have to know how a foreign country operates and how its people operate. Veterans have a unique perspective on other cultures that somebody who just graduated from college with no military experience and then went into the private sector would not have. Veterans definitely have an innovative and transformational value which they can bring to a company that cannot be taught in an academic setting.

Veterans, you need to know what your value is and maximize your skill set! Your training sets you apart from the non-veteran. It has a direct impact and direct civilian applications. It just needs to be rebranded to meet new requirements. Once you do that, businesses will definitely see the value that you bring to their company because they're looking at their bottom line. You have something that will improve their bottom line.

SECTION FOUR:
CORPORATE AMERICA'S "REAL SECRET SAUCE"

Why should businesses hire veterans? How can hiring a veteran make a business more profitable? A study conducted by the Syracuse University Institute for Veterans and Military Families reported, "Leadership ability and the strong sense of mission that comes from military service are characteristics that are highly valued in a competitive business environment." (Syracuse University 2012)

The report listed 10 points, and I'm going to go over each one.

1. Veterans are entrepreneurial.

Military training and socialization processes have been demonstrated to instill high levels of efficiency, trust, and a strong sense of comfort with autonomy and dynamic decision-making processes. These attributes are linked to entrepreneurship and an entrepreneurial mind-set engrained among military veterans and have been consistently demonstrated in practice. Veterans just need the knowledge and the right mentorship in how to establish a business, including how to gain the capital investment needed to begin their own business.

2. Veterans assume a high level of trust—the ability to trust co-workers and superiors.

Research studies focused on both military personnel and veterans indicate that the military service experience engenders a strong propensity toward an inherent trust and faith in co-workers and also a strong propensity toward trust in organizational leadership.

The hallmark of the military is trust in fellow soldiers as this is the only way to survive in a combat environment; soldiers have to trust in each other! An inherent trust in a co-worker, or more importantly an inherent trust in organizational leadership is crucial, as the most successful units have very successful and strong leaders who are highly respected and highly regarded by those they serve with. A commanding officer I served with in Afghanistan in 2012 comes to mind. I've previously mentioned him in an earlier chapter of this book. I respected this man not only because he was my military commanding officer, but because of the way he conducted himself and the way he treated the rank and file marines around him. He put in place an organizational leadership structure that made for a more cohesive unit, making the organization much more effective. He was the one who stressed doing everything in a legal, moral, and ethical manner. You will never go wrong with that. He set the example because he lived what he preached.

3. Veterans are adept at skills transfer.

The ability to recognize and act on opportunities to transfer skills learned in a specific context to a disparate context represents a valuable organizational resource. Several studies focused on skills transfer have highlighted that military service members and veterans are particularly adept at this ability. Research has attributed this finding to the fact that military training most often includes contingency and scenario-based training. As a result, service members and veterans develop cognitive heuristics that readily facilitate knowledge skills transfer between disparate tasks and situations.

Throughout my time in the military, veterans were always trained and did things on contingency and scenario-based training. All our training for infantry and all other specialties included scenario-based training. In preparation for deployment to Iraq and Afghanistan the vast majority of our training was scenario based, from the lowest tactical level to the highest strategic level. All ranks had to be trained according to a prescribed training doctrine before deployment.

4. Veterans have the ability to transfer skills from one occupational specialty to another—all to keep the mission moving forward. Veterans receive and leverage advanced technical training. Military experience on average exposes individuals to highly advanced technology and technological training at a rate that is accelerated relative to non-military age group peers.

Once you go through your military occupational training, you're always encouraged (and in many specialties required) to obtain additional training. Promotions are also education-based and service personnel are rewarded when they pursue additional educational training either via correspondence courses or by attending various educational courses at military installations. Training also includes advanced training in your occupational specialty as you advance in rank, or can be in different computer-based training programs depending on your rank and specialty. All military personnel have to be adaptable to the different technology and training methodologies that come through, especially as they relate to computer software. You have to adapt, as you move up in rank and position. You have to have the knowledge and also the ability and motivation to maintain a high degree of proficiency with the advanced technology inherent in the military.

With the advent of the War on Terror, military education has also evolved to extensively study the different cultures of the regions encountered by all military personnel assigned to the Middle East region. In each of my deployments the military had put together a comprehensive reading list and all military personnel were expected to read and become familiar with the region and the history of the Middle East. This has expanded into other areas of the globe. When military personnel travel to a given region you are expected to know the history and cultural nuances of that country. The armed forces today has many enlisted personnel who have gone on to college and have associate's degrees, bachelor's degrees, and higher.

5. Veterans are comfortable and able to adapt to changing environments.

The business environment can be dynamic and uncertain. Research consistently highlights the organizational advantage conferred to firms that are able to act quickly and decisively in the face of uncertainty and change. Cognitive and decision-making research has demonstrated that military experience is positively correlated to the ability to accurately evaluate a dynamic environment and act appropriately in the face of uncertainty. Several studies further highlight that this ability is enhanced and developed in individuals whose military experience has included service in a combat environment.

Veterans are highly trained to adapt to changing environments, and thus they tend to be very adaptable and resourceful. Veterans have to develop these skills as the modern battlefield is fluid and ever changing and you have to change with it to accomplish your mission. The old adage is the first plan changes with the first contact with the enemy. You have to be adaptable; there is no way around it! You have to be able to change when you encounter different environments; this was never more evident than was the case in Iraq and Afghanistan. The type of adaptability is inherent in a combat environment which is always changing and ever-evolving. When we went into Iraq in 2003 and Afghanistan in 2001, changes had to be made at the tactical, operational, and strategic levels as the war progressed, and we had to adapt to the dynamics of the combat environment.

Being able to adapt has never been more apparent than on the modern battlefield. Prior to the start of the war in Iraq, the military was trained in a purely conventional manner and as the conflict in Iraq and Afghanistan developed, military personnel had to evolve and adapt to the changing tactics of the enemy they were fighting. This included all ranks from the private to the general officer corps level.

6. Veterans exhibit high levels of resiliency.

The notion of resiliency refers to a condition where individuals can successfully adapt despite adversity, overcome hardships and trauma, achieve developmental competencies, and excel even in the face of harsh environments. Multiple studies have found that military veterans exhibit high levels of resilient behavior and that as a consequence of the military experience veterans generally develop an enhanced ability to come back from failed professional and/or personal experiences more quickly and more completely as compared to those who have not served.

This is a trait all veterans have. You have to adapt to the changing environment, especially in combat. Things don't always go right. You are going to fail at some things, but how you handle that failure will shape your character. All veterans have this character! Many times during my career in the Marine Corps, some things didn't go according to plan. I had to adapt and overcome the challenges before me. I failed at a few things, but failure brings success. Anybody who has succeeded has experienced failure; it's how you handle failure that will determine how you handle success. Veterans exhibit this high level of resiliency.

This was never more evident than when I started my business. I began with one set of assumptions and had to evolve with the changing nature of the business landscape. In business, you have to be adaptable to changing dynamics, consistently work to understand your customer base, work to understand how to leverage new business software, and always monitor your profit margin. Too often businesses fail because the owner did not recognize important changes or did not take appropriate action regarding new technology. Business owners who are adaptable thrive even in the uncertain economic environments of today's economy.

Veterans understand all too well the changing environment on the battlefield. The U.S. military had been trained to fight one way before Iraq and Afghanistan, but had to totally revamp their entire training, tactics, and procedure in fighting these new enemies—often on the fly.

A quote by President Theodore Roosevelt stresses this point. "It is not the critic who counts; not the man who points out how the strong man stumbles, or where the doer of deeds could have done them better. The credit belongs to the man who is actually in the arena, whose face is marred by dust and sweat and blood; who strives valiantly; who errs, who comes short again and again, because there is no effort without error and shortcoming; but who does actually strive to do the deeds; who knows great enthusiasms, the great devotions; who spends himself in a worthy cause; who at the best knows in the end the triumph of high achievement, and who at the worst, if he fails, at least fails while daring greatly, so that his place shall never be with those cold and timid souls who neither know victory nor defeat."

7. Veterans exhibit advanced team building skills.

Findings illustrate that when compared to those who have not served in the military, veterans are more adept with regard to 1) organizing and defining team goals and missions 2) defining team roles and responsibility and 3) developing a plan for action. Further research also suggests that those with prior military service have a higher level of efficiency for team related activities. That is, veterans exhibit an inherent and enduring belief that they can efficiently and effectively integrate and contribute to a new or existing team. Taken together, the academic research supports the notion that veterans will enable high-performing teams in an organizational setting to improve their performance.

Veterans are trained, no matter what branch of the armed forces they came from, to be able to work together as a team towards a common goal. Every section, every unit, company, platoon, squad, has to develop a team goal and mission. The passage of the Goldwater-Nichols Act in 1986 forced the armed forces into more joint operations, minimizing inter-service rivalry and making the armed forces work together for a common strategic purpose.

Everything is about reaching that common goal and working together. The most successful units are the ones that were able to integrate team building cohesion, and in this trait the veterans surpassed the non-veterans.

8. Veterans have strong organizational commitment.

Military institutions are particularly adept at institutional socialization. As a result, the military experience engenders a strong linkage between the individual and the organization. Research has demonstrated that military veterans bring a strong sense of organizational commitment and loyalty to the civilian workplace. For the organization, this strong sense of organizational commitment can contribute to reduced attrition and turnover and will also be reflected in the employees' work product. Further, in situations where organizational commitment is high, research suggests that organizational norms, customs, and ethical standards are strongly internalized and adopted across the firm.

Veterans tend to be more loyal to an organization than non-veterans. Throughout the armed forces, veterans hold loyalty to their unit, to their branch of the armed force, to each other, and to the group around them. As a Marine, I always think of myself as a Marine, even in retirement. There are no ex-Marines, just former Marines. My loyalty is to the Marine Corps! Inherently (and legally) all military personnel are loyal to the U.S. Constitution! All Marines have the same loyalty and it's the same with the other branches of the armed forces who exhibit a loyalty to their unit and organization.

9. Veterans have and leverage cross-cultural experiences.

The nature of military service today necessarily dictates that veterans must be skilled at operating across cultures and international boundaries. Multiple studies consistently show that those individuals with military backgrounds 1) have more international experience 2) speak more languages more fluently and 3) have a higher level of cultural sensitivity as compared to age-group peers that have not served in the military. The cross-cultural experiences characteristic of veterans represent a competitive advantage for the firm given the increasing globalization of the business environment.

The changing nature of the War on Terror has forced the military to adapt to the changing face of the modern battlefield. Before each deployment was made to a combat zone inside Iraq or Afghanistan all units had extensive cultural training for the region they were being sent to. Training included language, cultural norms, and culminated in a final field exercise in a mockup of a town with real role players playing fictional characters to be encountered. Scenario based training was set up at all levels having to meet certain objectives and each day evaluations were conducted to critique various units on how they responded during the exercise.

10. Veterans have experience and skill in diverse work settings.

The all-volunteer military actually represents a very heterogeneous workforce across a myriad of dimensions, including educational background, ethnicity, cultural values, and the goal aspirations of organizational members. As a consequence, multiple studies have found that those with military experience are, on average, highly accepting of individual differences in a work setting and exhibit a high level of cultural sensitivity with regard to such differences in the context of workplace interpersonal relationships.

Globalization Changes the Military

The knowledge of cross-cultural experiences has been a hallmark of the armed forces, especially today in the War on Terror. Prior to going into Iraq and Afghanistan, we didn't really have much of an idea of the cultural nuances of the Greater Middle East, North Africa, and the Central Asian Republic region. After 9/11, the military initiated cultural training.

When I deployed to Afghanistan and Iraq, I had to go through extensive cross-cultural training as part of my training as a Civil Affairs Marine. You have to learn the different cultures. You have to understand the languages. You have to understand how to negotiate in a cross-cultural environment. This is certainly the same case for many veterans as they go into Asia, Latin America, Africa, and Europe. You have to understand the cultural sensitivity of the country you're going into. For a business, in the global economy we're in, veterans understand and are more innovative when working with the different cultures. They understand the cultural differences between how Americans see things and how other cultures see them. The veteran is an untapped resource that businesses are not paying enough attention to. By tapping into that resource, they can ensure their businesses will become more profitable and have more stability and a lower attrition rate.

Syracuse University and Mackenzie and Company collaborated on a project in September 2012 that studied how companies might capture the distinctive capabilities that veterans can bring to civilian employers. (Syracuse University and Mackenzie and Company 2012)

Prime Quality Are Teamwork and Leadership

Accountability: Superior personnel and team accountability. Veterans understand how policies and procedures help an organization function. Veterans are more adapted to that. They understand the policies and procedures and can help make sure an organization runs smoothly.

Adaptability: Experiencing and operating in an ambiguous situation, exhibiting flexibility in fluid environments. The battlefield is ever-changing. The military is very adapted to changing with changing situations while still being able to accomplish the mission.

Team players: The ability to understand the capabilities and motivations of each individual regardless of background to maximize team effectiveness. The military veterans understand how to work together. They work with different individuals from different backgrounds—religious, ethnic, and now sexual orientation. As a result, the military is very adapted to working within changing environments.

Experienced leadership: Battle-tested leadership by leading from the front and leading by example. The ability to inspire devoted followership and lead groups to accomplish unusually difficult missions. Leadership starts from day one. As soon as you enter boot-camp you're taught to be a leader. You're taught to work together, but you're also taught that somebody's in charge and somebody leads. This has been happening with the wars in Iraq and Afghanistan. Former Marine Corps Commandant General Charles Krulakcame up with a concept of the strategic corporal, meaning that young Marines have to understand what the strategic concept is. If a soldier does something wrong, it could have strategic consequences. We've seen it on the battlefields in Iraq and Afghanistan.

The Second Aspect is Discipline

Self-reliance: Demonstrated initiative, ownership, and personal responsibility while leveraging all available assets and team members to ensure success. Self-reliance must work with initiative in taking personal responsibility. The hallmark of any soldier is this: if you make a decision, you are personally responsible for that decision, right or wrong. That's ingrained in you. There's a reason for that. You need personal responsibility. You don't want a leader who is going to pass the buck to somebody else if something goes wrong but take the credit when something goes right. Buck passing is not a trait that veterans tolerate. Political leaders all too often pass the buck and fail to take personnel responsibility for their actions and the consequences of those actions.

The recent crisis is Syria and Iraq has highlighted this as both Republican and Democrats do not want to take the tough stance and be committed to voting on whether they support or do not support military action being taken by the U.S. This is anathema to the military, as we are taught from the beginning of one's service to make a decision and stand by that decision. Politicians need to learn this!

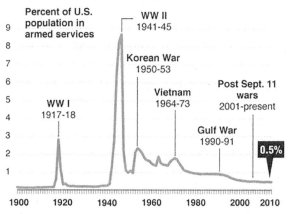

Figure 3: PEW Research Center Graph

Perseverance: Proven resilience, getting things done despite difficult conditions, tight deadlines, and limited resources. Veterans understand perseverance gets things done. In the wars in Iraq and Afghanistan and throughout my military career, you had to get things done under difficult conditions—all different circumstances and weather conditions. Combat epitomizes this. Deadlines have to be met and you are expected to get the job done. Most of the time you have limited resources and you're still supposed to accomplish the mission.

Strong work ethic: Belief in the value of hard work and taking the initiative. That's what the veteran does and that will be a valuable asset to any business.

Value driven: Proven experience, dedicating themselves to a cause. Veterans take pride in the mission and success of the organization. The biggest thing they did was they volunteered to serve their country. Many veterans over the last 12 or 13 years volunteered to go to war in Iraq and Afghanistan. I saw veterans repeatedly volunteer. They took pride in the mission and the success of their organization.

Solving Problems

Objective focused: Ability to organize and structure resources to accomplish the mission regardless of roadblocks. Any veteran can tell you that they faced many obstacles and roadblocks, but they were able to organize and structure their resource to accomplish the mission.

Quick-learners: Veterans have a proven ability to learn new skills quickly and efficiently. Veterans are taught from day one to get as much training as possible, to learn new skills, and apply those effectively to accomplish the mission. It would be an asset for any business to have an employee who is willing to learn new skills and use those skills to enhance the company's bottom line.

High-impact decision makers: Strong situational awareness is the ability to understand complex interdependencies and make decisions using practical judgment and creativity. Veterans are taught from the time they enter boot camp or officer training that they must learn how to make decisions. They must have the ability to understand what's going on and be able to make practical judgments and decisions in a complex, ever-evolving, and changing environment. As the leader, you have to make that decision and the buck stops with you

Diverse perspectives: Having experience with impacting and influencing people across the boundaries of cultural language, ethnicity, and personal motivation. Veterans have to deal with all types of individuals who come into the armed forces. There's no one-size fits all model—there are important differences. You have to deal with people from different cultures who will speak different languages and represent different ethnic groups. Everybody has personal motivations and you all have to work together to accomplish a common goal and mission.

Ten Hidden Facts about Veterans

Lida Citroen wrote an article for the business community in *Entrepreneur Magazine*. The article, written in July, 2014 is entitled, "Ten Things Veterans Want Hiring Managers to Know About Them".

1. The first thing is that talking about ourselves is uncomfortable. In the military, there is no I. Everything is focused on the group. We serve together. You don't put yourself above someone else. You don't take credit for something that everybody had a part in. Veterans have a hard time talking about themselves where it may be a little different in the private sector or civilian community. (Citroen 2014) Again, the first thing I learned early in my career was when something goes wrong you take the blame as a leader, but when something goes right give the credit to your men. The cardinal sin of any military veterans is to take unwarranted credit for something because humility is an honored trait that veterans take pride in. A trait that is very much ingrained into the Marine Corps culture is that the men under your command come first and foremost! As a leader you sleep last and get up first, you eat last and your lowest ranking Marine eats first, and everything is about placing your men first above your own comfort. Business leaders and political leaders need to understand this!

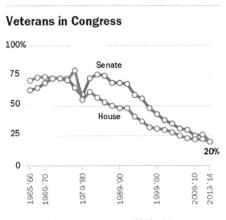

Figure 4: Vital Statistics: Veterans in Congress

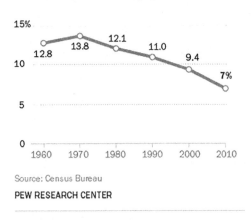

Figure 5: Census Bureau: Veterans as a share of population

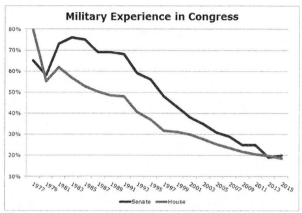

Figure 6: Source: Military Officers Association of America

2. Veterans come from a very structured environment. While serving, our work and our personal time are scheduled for us. We train on drills and scenarios giving us the power of preparedness. Everything is very structured in the military. From the way we organize ourselves to the way we follow through on things, we have respect for rules and we meet deliverables with efficiency. We adapt to new situations and are able to improvise when things aren't going the way they should.

3. Our spouses and families are an important part of our transition. For those who are leaving active duty, the family is the most important aspect of the process. Many veterans have gone through multiple relocations and excessive travel. They've worked long hours. These things are a standard part of the military. Some have been away for long periods because they were deployed to the various war zones in the Middle East. We try to balance work life and life with our spouses and families. But if a company is loyal to our family, they will have the undying loyalty of a veteran. They will have the buy-in without hesitation to that employee or that veteran.

4. Veterans resist the veteran label at work. We served out country in the military and now our career is over. We did that, done that, been there, but we don't want to keep hearing all the time that we're veterans. We appreciate the support we've been given, but we're not looking for a hand-out. That's the key issue here. Veterans *do not* want a hand-out or any type of welfare program. They just want to be given a chance to use the skills and training that they have.

5. We don't all have PTSD. This is a misconception. When you turn on the television and watch something that has to do with a veteran, the veteran is portrayed as having post-traumatic stress disorder. Not all veterans fall into that category. I think less than 20% of all veterans coming back from the wars in Iraq and Afghanistan have PTSD. What we don't want is to be labeled as "fragile" or "unstable".

6. We are used to stress and deadlines. The military epitomizes stress and deadlines. We operate under tight deadlines and pressure. We can think quickly on our feet and we have to be resilient to manage various crises, gather resources, and effectively make decisions. Many times this happens under sleep deprivation and exhaustion because we've worked long hours. There is no overtime pay. There is no set time. You're just expected to do it. As a leader in the military, you are expected to work long hours.

7. We are a mature workforce. While some of our counterparts might be immature, many veterans are battle-tested and focused. They're able to adapt to changing situations, and they're committed to the success of the organization. Maturity is a huge asset for employers seeking a dedicated workforce who can see through a problem and work it through to conclusion.

8. Company values are important to us. When you promote company values, mission, and vision, we will believe them until you prove otherwise. We have been trained to support the promotion of our values. We are trained to support the value of our unit, company, and organization. When a company says it believes in teamwork and supporting the community, the veteran expects the company to follow through with actions that show it is serious about it. Veterans mean it when they say they understand company values. They've been trained to do that in their career in the armed forces.

9. Some of us still serve. Many of us serve our country in the National Guard and the reserves. We know that time spent in our service might impact the company's work, but we will give you everything we have to make up for the lost time. We will give you everything we have to make sure your company succeeds. We're not looking for a handout! We're not looking for anything. If you understand that we're going to serve our country, we will definitely serve you and give 110%.

10. Many of us are unprepared for the transition from the military to civilian life. Since the wars in Iraq, millions have left the military. Many are struggling to relate to civilian hiring managers. Understanding how to market ourselves with personal branding, networking skills, and basic corporate nuances is important to us. We seek to present these resources so we can be evaluated more efficiently. We know we may be unprepared, but if you work with us, we will give you 110% of what we have to the organization or the company.

Enlightened Corporate Responsibility

Every year GI Jobs ranks the top 100 military-friendly companies (see Appendix A to view list), but not because these companies conduct business with the Department of Defense. The purpose of this listing is to highlight these companies because they invest in veterans and want them as part of their businesses. These companies consistently recruit veterans and understand the value they bring to their bottom line.

Forbes Magazine wrote an article that explained how these employers were chosen.

This ranking was published by *Forbes Magazine* in November 2013. The ranking is based on a comprehensive survey of over 100 questions compiled by an independent advisory board of industry experts. The survey assesses each company's long-term commitment to hiring those with prior military service, recruiting and hiring efforts and results, policies for reserve and National Guard members called to active duty, military spouse programs, and the presence of special military recruitment programs. The pool of companies eligible for the list is approximately 5,000 private sector companies with annual revenues of over $500 million per company. Only 2% of all eligible companies make the annual list of the top 100. This year's survey data were certified by Ernest & Young. (Smith 2013)

The Role of Universities

Colleges (see Appendix B to see list): *US Veterans Magazine* lists the top veteran-friendly schools in the country. (U.S. Veterans Magazine 2014)

Figure 7: Going on Patrol in Iraq

Figure 8: Training in Ramadi, Iraq

Figure 9: Army checkpoint in Ramadi, Iraq

SECTION FIVE:
BOOTS TO BUSINESS
Military Success for Veterans in Business

Dan Senor and Saul Singer wrote *Start-up Nation: the Story of Israel's Economic Miracle.* In the book they write about how the Israeli economy (or the Israeli private sector) embraced the military culture. Israeli companies want individuals to work for them who had a military background because they know the value of military service. The diversity, the innovation, the thinking on your feet, the austerity, all has a place to play in business and they just embrace this culture. Here in the United States it's the opposite. Most companies don't understand what a military background can bring or what military qualifications can bring to an entrepreneur wanting to start a new business.

Israeli entrepreneur Jon Medved—who has sold several startups to large American companies—told us, "When it comes to U.S. military resumes, Silicon Valley is illiterate. It's a shame. What a waste of the kick ass leadership talent coming out of Iraq and Afghanistan. The American business community has no idea what to do with them."

Senor and Singer wrote that the gulf between business and the military is symptomatic of a wider divide between America's military and the civilian communities it has sworn to protect.

Leading From the Front

In the military, as soon as you enter boot camp or attend an officer training course, you are instilled with the idea that you are in charge, meaning you are in charge of all personnel and equipment. This is the first thing and the most repeated concept which is instilled into you. In any situation where a group of military personnel are located, someone will be in charge, and at any given time that could be you! When you are in charge, you're in charge! College doesn't teach how to think like this! With all the pressure and high stakes, you're forced to think, three or four moves ahead. They don't teach this in college! College teaches you academics and theories, the military teaches life experience at a practical real world strategic level! The military gives you practical experience which is invaluable to any business organization.

This is what businesses should be embracing! This is why veterans make the perfect entrepreneurs and business owners. This "can do" attitude works on the battlefield and it works in business. The military is much better than college at inoculating young leaders with this concept. The people you are serving with come from all walks of life. The military is a purely merit-based institution. Learning how to deal with anybody no matter where they come from is something that should be leveraged in today's business.

Proven Combat Leadership

On April 25, 2014, the television station WJLA, an ABC news affiliate in Washington, DC, ran a story titled "Why Do Veterans Make the Best Entrepreneurs?"

When most people think of an entrepreneur, they imagine someone born with business in their bones. For example, individuals like Steve Jobs revolutionized our world in many ways. The truth of the matter is that entrepreneurship can be taught and learned, assuming you're mentally ready to make the jump. In addition, if you're a US military veteran then you already possess many of the skills that make successful entrepreneurs—well—successful. The WJLA story asked the question: What do revolutionary entrepreneurs like Sergey Brin, Jeff Bezos, Elon Musk and the late Steve Jobs have in common with US military veterans?

- Both groups exhibited traits such as:

- A high-tolerance for ambiguity

- The stomach to take risks

- A high degree of self-confidence

- Overly optimistic outlooks

- Relying extensively on their own intuition

Veterans are trained to control the fear of failure. Failure is a part of business. Not everything goes smoothly; it's not likely you are going to be the one who will invent the greatest product. The tenacity is what is going to get you through, so you need to control your fear. Veterans are trained how to control this fear of failure and still accomplish the mission.

The No Fear Factor

Veterans are well trained and have the ability to adapt to changing conditions. (O'Donnell 2014). The war in Iraq is a prime example. The military entered the War on Terror prepared to fight against a conventional opponent. The strategic plan was based on the strategy employed during the Persian Gulf War of 1990-91. Unfortunately the enemy has its own strategies and did not respond the way we had trained for. The assumptions we used as we entered the conflict in Iraq and Afghanistan had to be adjusted and changed, plus the fear of change had to be overcome as the strategic military strategists had to adjust to the new realities on the ground.

Combat is never portrayed realistically by Hollywood. All veterans who enter combat have fear, the fear of being killed or wounded, the fear of letting your fellow members down, the fear of not measuring up to your comrades, and the fear of not being able to do what you have been trained to do. We all have fear, it's how you handle that fear, how you may have fear to move, but you move forward anyway. Veterans may have fear of how they will handle a given combat situation, but they still go anyway. They still volunteered anyway when they could have easily have taken a less dangerous occupation. Yet they still went into the breach to fight anyway when all their civilian counterparts stayed safe at home while they chose to go to the sounds of conflict. This is what a veteran can bring to a business and what a veteran can bring to their own business.

I experienced this fear when the marketing firm I originally hired failed to deliver what they had promised, and I had to change directions. Would I be successful, would I be able to reconstruct my business, did I make a mistake in moving to Tampa, away from family and friends? Fear has to be controlled and channeled into more constructive pursuits as you continue to drive forward. This is what I learned in the military: never quit, never surrender to your fear, and keep driving forward!

Not everything goes correctly. You're going to make mistakes; you're going to stumble along the way. But a business owner is the one who strives to make it happen. He's going to make mistakes; he's not going to listen to the critics or naysayers. When I started my business, everybody told me, "No, you can't make it. There's no way you can do that." So if you listen to them, you're just going to be like the other doubting Thomases. You will never succeed if you listen to the critics because they aren't taking the risks like you are.

Veterans and entrepreneurs understand taking of risks!

The Zen Master

The other aspect veterans understand is "the planning process." The military planning process could be equated to the business planning process. You need to know everything about your business. You need to know who are your adversaries and competitors. You need to know everything about yourself—your capabilities and your assets.

To quote Sun Tzu, "If you know the enemy and know yourself, you need not fear the result of a hundred battles. If you know yourself but not the enemy, for every victory gained you will also suffer a defeat. If you know neither the enemy nor yourself, you will succumb in every battle."

The military planning process is the same as the business planning process. You have to be organized. You have to know the A to Z of how you're going to organize your business. You need to know A to Z how you're going to plan your business and how you're going to sell your business. What are your strengths? What are your weaknesses? How are you going to fund it? What employees are you going to have? If you are going to be a brick and mortar business, where will it be located? Everything you know is in that business plan. The military understands the planning process. That's why veterans make outstanding entrepreneurs because they understand how to plan and plan for success.

1, 2, 3 and Off to the Races

In *Entrepreneur Magazine,* on May 23, 2014, Jeff Weiss wrote three things you need to know when you start your business—

1. Have a plan.

    I'm going to go into this a little bit later on how I started my business and the mistakes and successes I learned over time.

2. Find a mentor:

    A mentor is crucial to the establishment of your business, especially for veterans. You may not have the knowledge to start a business. You may not have the background to start a business. Make sure when you enlist the help of a mentor the person has high ethical and moral standards. There are sharks out there and I had to learn this the hard way; I do not want other veterans to deal with that problem.

3. Hire employees as soon as possible:

    Too often we wait until we get everything aligned. The first thing you need to do is hire employees because you can't be an expert in everything. Hire somebody, give them the directions, have it set up and know what they're going to do, what they're going to accomplish, and what their position will be. Have it organized and this person can help you grow the business as you grow over time. While avenues of opportunity for veterans abound there are many resources you can find through the web and the Small Business Administration. There are a lot of resources out there. One thing you need to understand is that those you have served with are among the most loyal and dedicated workers you could have. If you can get a business and you can establish it by hiring and working with other veterans that you served with, you already know what they can do. You just need to be organized and have a dedicated list of what they're going to do and what they're going to provide for the business.

Getting Your Business Started

As I stated previously, I'm now going to go into how I've set up my business, how I run it, and the mistakes and successes I made in the beginning.

1. Why would you want to run your own business?

The first thing I wanted was to be my own boss, to be able to do it my way and not be constrained by others. This way I could make my own schedule, and put what I wanted to do into the business. I worked at a political consulting firm; I love politics, it is my passion! But I always felt constrained and overruled even though I was often correct in my judgments. I decided to be my own boss so I could do things my way and turn a passion into a profit orientated business.

2. How do military skills translate into a business?

You know operational planning. You know how to set up a plan. You know how to organize things. Veterans know the planning process and have learned to plan effectively for all types of contingencies. You have to look at everything from A to Z of the operation, from logistics to organization to command and control to execution. Operational planning goes hand-in-hand in business.

3. Initiative—you need to be innovative

You need to have initiative if you're going to take a risk. You need to take risks. I recall one thing I was told when I was putting together my business plan. A friend who kept looking at my business plan kept mentioning that even though I might have the perfect business plan, but eventually I would have to take a risk. That's where initiative comes in. Someone opening up a business has to have the ability to overcome challenges, I made mistakes along the way because I had never set up a business before, and I didn't know how to do it. I knew about getting a license and the legal requirements, but there's more to starting a business than getting the paperwork completed.

I had to overcome challenges, and the biggest one was hiring a marketing firm. I had vetted a marketing firm and unfortunately it was the wrong marketing firm, as they over-promised but underperformed on results.

4. Adaptability

Business owners have to be adaptable. Things change. You've got to change with them. You've got to try to recognize the changes that are coming before they arrive. Many businesses across the country failed because they refused to adapt or were unable to adapt to changing market forces or new technological advancements. You have to be able to be organized and understand time management—veterans understand this. You have to be a leader just like you were in the military; you have to be a leader while you're in business. Then the question becomes why did I start my own business? Having worked at a political consulting firm, I saw the way they did things and I knew I could do things differently. I knew I could do things better. I knew there was a market for what I wanted to try to do. I wanted to do something that I loved, but do it the way I wanted.

5. The skills and education you need to start a business.

It all depends on what type of business you have. If you want a consulting firm for example, maybe you should have a college degree. You need expertise, which you can acquire or hire. Some businesses don't require a college degree. You just need the ability to be adaptive, take the initiative, and take the risk. You also need to find out if your idea, your passion, can be successful. Most businesses just need guts! You just need to take the risk. If you have a passion for something, then follow that passion and develop a business which makes use of that passion.

6. Life experiences.

Maybe you've experienced something, but you could do something better. There's a way to start a business, change the prevailing theme and do something different that'll benefit a consumer or group. Do something different. Many businesses have started because they took a concept and made it even better. This could be something you could start with a spouse. Tap into the resources and experience of your spouse, as they are an excellent source since they have been part of your military career. Now they can be part of the next phase of your life.

7. What preparations are needed for starting a business?

The key is you've got to do your research. You start with a passion, but passion is not enough. This is where the business planning or, for veterans, the military planning process comes in. You need to research your opposition. What competition is out there? What are they doing? What are their strengths and weaknesses? Then you can incorporate that into your business to see what direction you need to go. Previous employment and military duty assignments help in starting a business. Every job you held or every duty assignment that you have served in the military can be useful to help you start your business. Previous employments help you gain experience, and that helps you gain knowledge. It all helps you find a way to make your business successful. Military service is paramount because that's where you learn to take the biggest risks. In combat, you have to take big risks. It takes a certain individual to go over the berm with a rifle and charge the enemy. It takes risk to go into combat, to lead men into battle.

8. What do I need to know to successfully transition to civilian life?

Currently, I am working and starting the Vet Transition Academy to help other veterans avoid some of the pitfalls I encountered. The Vet Transition Academy will guide and help military veterans with starting their businesses and teaching them how to execute their business models. Far too often organizations give you information on how to begin your business, but information only goes so far. The Vet Transition Academy not only gives you the information, but will mentor you in taking your business concept all the way through to execution and implementation.

9. What type of business should I start?

What are you most passionate about? What are your interests? Leveraging technology and starting a business with the internet, computers, and all the things that go with it, if you're technologically savvy, is one way to go. Then you have to decide where you want to live once you transition out of the military. I was living in Sacramento, but decided it would be better to relocate to Tampa, Florida which fit perfectly with my business model. Tampa offered what California could not, a place to re-establish my business because of the military friendliness of the state and the pro-business nature of Florida.

The Reservist

For my reserve service, and for those in the reserves, you're taking time away from your family or your civilian job to serve in the military. It takes a certain kind of individual to do that. It's the same on active duty. I served in both the reserves and active duty and the experience I gained in both was invaluable to me as I began my business venture. I got to see many reservists who had their own businesses. I got to meet a lot of active duty military personnel and see how they did things, learn about leadership, learn about how they lead men, and learn how they plan things. Service in Iraq and Afghanistan is a valuable asset in starting a business! You had to be innovative during your time of military service. The dedication, the long hours, everything that goes into serving in a combat zone pays dividends in a business. During my military service I met many different people from different cultures, and understanding different regions of the world from their perspectives factored into the establishment of my business.

As a reservist I worked in the private sector and observed many aspects of life in the political and business environment and in each case it helped shape a conceptual understanding of the business I have created and am now part of.

Challenging Washington

Currently, I own a political media company, which deals with national and international issues; my experience in the military has been a critical asset. Having served in various overseas deployments, I know the different cultures in the different regions of the world. Military service gave me a much broader perspective. The education I gained from my Bachelor's degree in government, my Master's degree in National Security Studies, and my concentration in Middle East studies has paid dividends in the business that I established.

Not every business needs a Bachelor's or a Master's degree. It all depends what you want to do. Bill Gates dropped out of college and started Microsoft. Many of the top business leaders in the nation do not have college degrees. It helps, but it's not necessary in starting a business—or growing a very successful business.

If you have a technical or vocational background, there are many businesses which can be very lucrative. It depends on what business you're getting into, but even if you're getting into a business where you need a college education, additional vocational and technical experience will definitely boost your chances of success even more. Not only that, they will also give you more insight into your academic studies.

While working at a political consulting firm I realized I wanted to start my own business and do things differently. Of all my previous experience, the most valuable was my service in the armed forces, as this gave me a strategic understanding of global and domestic politics.

I began Ubaldi Reports in 2014; previously my company was called Military Briefing Book. The business model was the same, the change was instead of posting articles from different media and political think tanks, Ubaldi Reports would be a site in which I would be the primary writer. As the company grew I would hire military veterans who had experience on domestic and global issues as my staff writers.

While on deployment to Afghanistan, I realized I needed to change directions. I was always contemplating changing it or doing something different because it wasn't reaching the intended target audience I had in mind. I realized you cannot be tied to a static business model; you have to be adaptable and accept change!

My business experience began after I left the political consulting firm. A close friend who owned a business asked, "What do you like and what are you passions?" Everybody that I know and who knows me knows my passion is politics. So why not do something that involves politics? That's a good idea, but where do I start? Then another friend said he would be interested in a site that had commentary from someone who served in Iraq and Afghanistan. That's how I started Military Briefing Book which was a business about national and international issues and military related topics. Then I realized, as the wars were receding, Americans were more concerned about what was happening here at home. So, I changed the name to Ubaldi Reports. Now I'm reporting on national and international issues that impact Americans here at home. I'm doing the writing, conducting the research, and putting it up on my website, providing an independent voice on domestic and international issues, but one that is written by veterans who served in the U.S. armed forces.

Before you start your business, you have to figure out how you're going to get funding. I saved every dollar I made while I served in Afghanistan and Iraq, especially in my last deployment. This provided the funding I needed to overhaul my business. Because I had saved money, I was able to hire a marketing firm to help keep me organized and expand my business, giving me a national presence. The problem was that I went with the wrong marketing company. I hired a national marketing firm that had a prominent individual running it and who was very well known. As time went on, I found they over-promised and under-delivered. In business, it is critical that you thoroughly check out companies you will be dealing with. Mistakes can be costly for many reasons.

Now you have to remember that being a veteran has little practical benefits beyond the fact that the public supports you. There are pitfalls involved in starting and running a business; you have to organize your business from the beginning, from before the beginning actually. Get the right advice, but not from individuals who are predisposed against your idea. Too many people would come up and would say, "Well, I don't like politics, but I would do this." Individuals would say they dislike politics but always give me suggestions on what they would like all the while having a total anathema against my business model.

Make sure you only take advice from those who advocate doing everything legally, ethically, and morally. They should have your best interests at heart. You must be careful because many companies only want your money and give you little practical business advice to help you execute your business.

Pitfalls in Business

I made many mistakes along the way because I didn't have the knowledge of how to start a business. I didn't know what to do. I was making many mistakes. One of them was hiring a marketing firm. What you need, as I said earlier, is the *right* mentor. Make sure your mentor is a good mentor who has strong ethics, is sound morally, and will do things honestly. He's looking to help you out, not help himself out. It's somebody who has your best interests in mind. My current mentor really engaged and challenged me on my assumptions. You have to be receptive. You cannot be thin-skinned when you're in business. A good mentor should challenge your assumptions and keep you organized and a good mentor should be somebody who has many years in business and can help guide you to where you need to go.

Another of the mistakes that I made was hiring the wrong web designer. A person should know everything about your business to help you design your website. Anyone can design a website, but you want the right design, which will make your company stand out from your competition. You need to select the right

SEO (search engine optimization) company. This company will optimize your company by helping you get a strong web presence by inserting key words and all the other aspects which go into giving you a strong presence. This company has to be different from your social media as Google and Facebook are continuously changing the rules and you need to stay updated.

The optimization of your website is crucial in expanding your business to reach your target audience. It all depends on what type of business you're going into. For my business, I needed to be optimized on a national level. My first SEO operator didn't optimize my website properly and now I have a better SEO operator who is guiding my website to reaching a greater audience. You have to ask the right questions, and they should know your business in and out just like you do.

A social media presence is crucial today in the era of Facebook, Twitter and all the other social media platforms. A business needs to work with a company that truly understands the concept of how social media integrates with business. My previous marketing company did not provide the right social media concept and gave me wrong information on how I should utilize social media for my company. When I meet my current social media team they have given me invaluable information which has increased my social media presence. Social media and SEO optimization is not a onetime expense but a continuous process.

Proper time management is where my mentor is helping me out—making sure that I'm organized and that I'm not all over the place. Just like in the military, every business needs to organized and kept on task!

Whom do you associate with when you begin your business? Again, this goes back to the importance of associating with individuals who have strong ethics and morals to help you with your business. Be careful because there are a lot of unscrupulous marketers. There are a lot of unscrupulous business people out there who will try to influence you for their benefit and not yours.

These are some of the reasons I wanted to set up the Vet Transition Academy. I want to be able to instruct veterans on how to establish a business, to warn them about the mistakes I've made and how I've learned from them. I also want to guide them in the correct way so they're not wasting their money and their time. There are many ways to start a business; these are some of the highlights. At the Vet Transition Academy, veterans will learn how to start a business and be organized, and most importantly, they will learn how to execute their businesses as they move forward.

SECTION SIX:
AMERICA'S JEDIS

How many of us really understand the quality of veterans serving today?

The veterans today are an untapped resource and are not being utilized effectively in the United States.

We live at a time when participation in the military or any connection to the military is at its lowest level.

On December 8, 1941, President Roosevelt speaking to a Joint Session of Congress just after the attack on Pearl Harbor stated, "December 7, 1941—a date which will live in infamy—" From this pronouncement the entire nation mobilized to defeat a common foe.

The "Next Greatest Generation" Goes to War

September 11, 2001 was an equally transformational event in the history of the United States, where the nation's homeland was attacked. Instead of our military being attacked, the nation as a whole was attacked and our citizens killed. In a Joint Secession of Congress shortly after the terror attack on the nation, President Bush stated, "Americans are asking: What is expected of us? I ask you to live your lives, and hug your children. I know many citizens have fears tonight, and I ask you to be calm and resolute, even in the face of a continuing threat."

The American public did was what was asked of it, as the flag of this country flew so proudly all across the country in defiance against those who committed this horrific act. For months the American people flew the nation's flag, as millions of Americans were seeking to punish the perpetrators. After this horrific event President Bush, with authorization from Congress, committed the United States to War; the unfortunate aspect is that the nation did not go to war, only the military went off to war. Unlike World War II, there was no conscription, there was no shared sacrifice, there was no rationing of basic commodities as was the case in World War II. Over time the military would experience sustained combat operations in Iraq and Afghanistan and throughout the Middle East Region, but as time passed, the flags slowly came down and the partisan politics of pre-September 11th returned. It's interesting to note while serving on active duty only months after September 11th another senior Marine and I were discussing the renewed patriotism of America, when he stated, "Watch as the country becomes far removed from the attack, the flags will come down and the country will return to the way it was before we were attacked." The nation's consciousness is short lived and only those in the armed forces knew this would be a generational struggle.

Two Separate Societies

Thirteen years later America again remembered that horrific event, but unlike the generation which went off to war in World War II with the full support of the American people, America after September 11th didn't mobilize—didn't sacrifice! The only sacrifice felt by the American people was when they went through airport security with its intrusive screening process.

Co-writing in the *New York Times,* former Lieutenant General Karl Eikenberry and David Kennedy wrote, "These developments in recent decades have widened this chasm. First and most basic was the decision in 1973, with the end of combat operations in Vietnam, to depart from the tradition of the citizen soldier by ending conscription and establishing a large, professional, all-volunteer force to maintain the global commitments we have assumed since WWII. In 1776, Samuel Adams warned of the dangers inherent in such an arrangement. A standing army, however necessary it may be at some times, is always dangerous to the liberties of the people. Soldiers are apt to consider themselves as a body distinct from the rest of the citizens."

Eikenberry & Kennedy continued, "For nearly two decades, no American has been obligated to serve and few do. Less than .5% of the population serves in the armed forces compared with more than 12% during WWII, even fewer of the privileged and powerful shoulder arms. In 1975, 70% of members of Congress had some military service. Today just 20% do and only a handful of their children are in uniform."

In 1982, when I enlisted in the Marine Corps, the WWII generation, as Tom Brokaw famously wrote in his book labeled as *The Greatest Generation*, were nearing retirement or retiring, as they had reached the mandatory age of 65. When I went off to war in Iraq and Afghanistan fewer and fewer of the U.S. civilian population had any connection to the military or had served themselves. When I deployed to Afghanistan in 2002, a friend in my church told me that she did not know anyone serving in the military, let alone someone in Afghanistan. We are beginning to have a system where the military is becoming more distant and isolated from the public they are sworn to protect.

In 2009, we had a horrific tragedy at Fort Hood, where U.S. Army psychiatrist Major Nidal Malik Hasan fatally shot and killed 13 individuals and wounded a dozen others. I was asked to give a briefing to the media and found that none of the media affiliates had any knowledge of military life or the conditions on a military base. The questions I was asked by the press were very basic and would have been unheard of only a generation ago.

Warrior/Civilian Chasm

I was reminded of two events which demonstrate the situation in America. The first one was in 2004, when one of the TV commentators made a comment during President Ronald Reagan's funeral procession down Pennsylvania Avenue. The commentators were viewing the procession of U.S. military personnel marching in formation when the host stated this was probably the first time many Americans had seen the military march in their lifetime.

The second incident took place at the one year anniversary of September 11th while I was stationed at Bagram Airfield in Afghanistan. An American reporter asked me a very basic question on what position a Captain in the Army would hold? A generation before this would have been easily understood!

I was reminded recently at my retirement ceremony that many in the audience came to support my retirement and were amazed at the ceremony and the professionalism of the Marines taking part in the ceremony. The unfortunate aspect was many in attendance had never been in the military, been on a military base, and are far removed from anyone in their family who served, with many going back to a grandfather or great-grandfather serving in a far distant conflict only known to history.

This illustrated a stark contrast to the difference between those who serve and those who do not. We currently have a division in American society between the non-veterans and veterans who do not understand each other. On November 13, 2010, Lieutenant General John Kelly addressed the Semper Fi Society of St. Louis just days after learning his son had been killed in Afghanistan.

"Most wearing the eagle, globe, and anchor today join the unbroken ranks of American heroes after that fateful day, not for money or promises of bonuses or travel to exotic liberty ports, but for one reason and one reason alone. Because of the terrible assault on our way of life. Men they knew must be killed and the extremist ideology destroyed. A plastic flag in their car window was not their response to the murderous assault on our country. No, their response was a commitment to protect the nation by swearing an oath to their God to do so to their deaths. When future generations ask why America is still free while the heyday of al Qaeda and their terrorist allies was counted in days rather than centuries as the extremists themselves predicted, our hometown heroes, soldiers, sailors, airmen, Coast Guardsmen, and Marines can say, "because of me and people like me who risked all to protect millions, who will never know my name."

General Kelly continued, "America's civilian and military protectors, both here at home and overseas, have for nearly nine years fought this enemy to a standstill and have never for a second wondered why. They know and are not afraid. Their struggle is our struggle. They hold in disdain those who claim to support them and not the cause that takes their innocence, their limbs, even their lives. As a democracy, we the people, and that means every one of us, sent them away from home to fight our enemies. We are all responsible. I know it doesn't apply to those here tonight, but if anyone thinks you can somehow thank them for their service and not support the cause for which they fight—America's survival, then they are lying to themselves and rationalizing away something in their lives. More importantly, they are slighting our warriors and mocking their commitment to the nation."

General Kelly made one final bold statement, "It is a fact that our country today is in a life-and-death struggle against an evil enemy, but America as a whole is certainly not at war. Not as a country, not as a people. Today, only a tiny fraction, less than 1%, shoulders the burden of fear and sacrifice, and they shoulder it for the rest of us. Their sons and daughters who serve are men and women of character who continue to believe in this country enough to put life and limb on the line without qualification, without thought of personal gain. They serve so that the sons and daughters of the other 99% don't have to. No big deal. Though as Marines (and as the other branches: Army, Navy, Air Force, and

Coast Guard) have always been the first to fight, paying in full the bill that comes with being free for everyone else."

Alien Nation

Everyone rationalizes why they choose not to serve. Many, looking at military service through the partisan prism of politics, reiterate it's only the power elites in Washington who send the military off to war. I would expand this and take a much broader view. Society as a whole is influenced by many factors, not just the power elites, but from all sides of the political spectrum: those sitting in academia, how the military is covered by the media, and finally how the entertainment industry portrays the military and veterans. This is a far different characterization than the veterans of World War II.

Many places around the country look at military service as advocating war, San Francisco refused to have the battleship Iowa home ported at its pier as a World War II museum, stating they were not about to commemorate war but want to be known for peace. That's like saying the military does not want peace! Even George Washington stated, "The surest way to preserve peace is to prepare for war." How many colleges and universities around the country have viable ROTC programs on their campuses? Many Ivy League colleges and universities are just beginning to reinstate ROTC back into their campus after a forty year absence. Still university presidents and those in academia around the country often show disdain toward the military and the ethos which is embedded into each veteran.

It seems Duty, Honor, and Commitment should be cherished instead of reviled. Maybe if the values cherished by veterans were instilled throughout the country, we would not have had the financial collapse in 2008-09, or the dysfunction permeating America's government at all levels.

As the World War II generation passes from the scene, this trend will only intensify, as fewer students will have had grandparents,

parents, or siblings serving in the military, and so their knowledge about this vital institution will come from the media or from professors, who are even less likely to have a military connection. (Feaver 2014)

The root of the problem is clear in the statistics; less than one percent of Americans are serving in the Armed Forces. Of those who have not served themselves, only a tiny percentage has direct connections to the military through family, friends, or coworkers. Under the draft, a wider cross section of society served in the military, and those who would not have otherwise joined were able to experience military life and carry it back to their civilian careers. Today many Americans do not know anyone who serves and are likely to feel disconnected because they do not understand what the military is, what it is doing, and how its activities affect their lives. (Skelton 2012)

The military culture of duty, honor, courage, and commitment is an alien concept to many in American society, especially among leading elected officials, but it is the hallmark and ethos of all military personnel who have served. Military personnel are taught from the very beginning of their training that giving your word and integrity are two of the central principles of military service. Unfortunately today, these characteristics are often reviled instead of cherished. Washington should learn this!

Washington's Lack of Military Experience

The American public is being systematically alienated from the very individuals who wear the uniform of those serving in the armed forces of the United States. This is most apparent when we look at the lack of veterans serving in Congress. With the military conducting operations in Afghanistan and now with ongoing operations in Iraq and Syria, too many are far removed from those who will actually be called on by the country to serve in these forbidding regions. Most Americas view the images, but then move on with their lives, not understanding or being connected to those who will be called to do the nation's bidding. Many in Congress, the President, and the administration are advocating deeper military action in Syria, but how many personally know someone in their immediate family who is serving in the armed forces of this country today?

The *St. Louis Post-Dispatch* on May 26, 2014, reported, "Currently about 20% of representatives and senators have served in the military." According to numbers compiled by the House Armed Services Committee and the American Legion, in 1976, Legion records show 77% were veterans.

The *Post-Dispatch* continued to report, "The dwindling number of vets is one of the biggest changes in Congress over the last 40 years—a direct reflection of the end of the draft in 1973 and the resulting smaller percentage of veterans in the general population."

As Veterans of Foreign Wars' Public Affairs Director Joe Davis, points out, 16 million Americans served in WWII, more than 12% of the nation's population of 132 million. The year before the country entered the war. Less than 1% of the current population of 317 million served in Iraq or Afghanistan.

The congressional peak for veterans came right after Vietnam. In 1977, according to numbers compiled by the American Legion, 347 of 435 members of the House and 65 of 100 senators were veterans. The number of Senate veterans peaked at 73 in 1981. (Raasch 2014)

In its July 14, 2014 report titled, *Membership of 113th Congress: a Profile,* The Congressional Research Service reported, "At the beginning of the 113th Congress, there were 108 members. Twenty percent of the total membership had served or were serving in the military. This was 10 fewer than at the beginning of the 112th Congress with 118 members, and 20 fewer than in the 111th Congress with 128 members.

According to the list compiled by Congressional Quarterly Roll Call, the House currently has 88 veterans including two female members as well as two delegates. The Senate has 18. These members served in WWII, the Korean War, the Vietnam War, the Persian Gulf War, Afghanistan, Iraq, and Kosovo, as well as during times of peace. Many have served in the reserves and in the National Guard. Eight House members and one Senator are still serving in the reserves. Six House members are still serving in the National Guard. Both the female House members are combat veterans.

The number of veterans in the 113th Congress reflects the trend of steady decline in recent decades in the number of members who have served in the military. For example, 64% of the members who served in the 97th Congress (1982-1982) were veterans. In the 92nd Congress (1971-1972), 73% of the members were veterans. (Manning 2014)

Tom Brokaw, interviewed in April 2009, said, "Regarding the returning veterans of WWII, employers thought that there must be something wrong with the applicant if he didn't serve their country in WWII." This characterized many employers who honored veterans over non-vets looking for private sector jobs. When I left my position in 2007, one of my greatest disadvantages was that I was veteran. I had served my country and, most importantly, I was an active reservist. Companies didn't want to hire me because they thought and feared I would be activated. How sad it is that we don't want to hire our veterans.

Earth & Mars Not Aligned

Colonel Peter Mansoor wrote the book *Baghdad at Sunrise.* He was one of the leading military experts for General Petraeus during the surge of U.S. forces into in Iraq. Mansoor made a stunning observation in the last chapter of his book.

"Fifteen months after my return from Iraq, I was invited to a cocktail reception on the Upper East Side of Manhattan. After discovering that the son of the host and hostess was interested in military affairs, I suggested that since the US Military Academy was just up the river from New York City, perhaps he should consider applying for admission. The hostess interrupted us, put her arm around her son's shoulder and replied, 'No, no, no, no, no. He has much more important things planned for his life.' She then patted me on the arm and said, 'But I'm glad we had people like you to protect us'.

"How sad that people like them are waiting for "people like us" to protect them," Mansoor concluded. People say that it's only the wealthy who protect their kids and send everybody else's children off to war. I would like to broaden that out to the greater part of society. How many of those in the media, academia, or the business community have a son or daughter serving?

When I returned from duty in Iraq, I was invited by my brother to celebrate Thanksgiving at the home of his wife's family in Southern California. Since I was stationed nearby at Camp Pendleton, and only weeks removed from Iraq it was a nice change of pace to be somewhere else than on a military base for the holiday. His in-laws did all the traditional things one would expect of any family across the country on Thanksgiving, and football was part of that tradition. After the game was over and everyone was relaxing after the feast of Thanksgiving, I was asked if I flew there to visit my brother I stated that no, I was in the Marines stationed at Camp Pendleton, and just recently returned from duty in Iraq. The host got all excited and called everyone over so they could ask me numerous questions, as they had never met anyone who served in Iraq or Afghanistan. This would have been unheard of during World War II, as everyone knew someone serving.

As time passes, Americans are increasingly failing to understand the basic concepts of their own history. How thoroughly do we teach our children what transpired in WWII? We watch the movies, documentaries, and kids today even play video games based on World War II themes, but how many of us truly understand the battles and the conflicts our veterans fought to preserve what we have today? Do we discuss the values of military service to our children in elementary school, middle school, and high school? As they enter college, do we teach them military history or is it only a footnote?

It's interesting how many in American society know very little of American military history. Just recently I was helping a friend with preparations in celebrating her grandfather's 100th birthday. He served in five major military campaigns in Europe during the Second World War, beginning with the landings at Normandy, and had fought in the Ardennes military campaign, better known as the Battle of the Bulge. I explained to her that her grandfather served in one of the deadliest battles of the war with one the greatest losses of American military lives, reminiscent of many of the battles during the U.S. Civil War. How often is military history incorporated into the U.S. educational curriculum? Many colleges and universities barely even broach the subject. Recognizing this can help us understand why Americans have such little understanding of our own past. Many tend to focus on other educational pursuits and not focus on military battles as it seems they feel they are glorifying war. This is far from the truth!

Whether you're liberal, conservative, Republican or Democrat, I must ask: how do you look at a veteran? Do you look at a veteran with contempt or find some reason to debase the military? Or do you look at veterans as men and women to look up to? Would you want one of your sons or daughters to become members of the United States Armed Forces?

A Father's Story

I am reminded of a book authored by Frank Schaeffer titled *Keeping Faith: A Father-Son Story About Love and the United States Marine Corps*. It is a memoir of a man and the conflicting emotions he felt when he learned that one of his sons had decided to enlist in the Marines Corps. The elder Schaeffer said he was taken aback when his son announced he was joining the Marines.

"My friends were sending their sons and daughters to top colleges," the father said during a summer speech at the Military Child Education Coalition conference in Groton, Conn.

"I never served in the military," he observed. "Our kind, highly educated denizens of the North Shore, rarely enlist these days."

His son's decision to join the Marines made it harder for the elder Schaeffer to face his friends. "So where is John going to college?" was the question he said he didn't relish answering from parents who were itching to tell me all about their sons or daughters who were going to Harvard.

Shaeffer noted that in 1999 his son was the only senior graduating from the Waring School, an elite prep school in Beverly, Mass who considered military service, Schaeffer said one perplexed mother asked him, "But aren't the Marines terribly Southern?"

"What a waste, he was such a good student," said another parent.

This rationale stunned Schaeffer as he realized we support the military and all they do, but only as long as it's someone else's child. Are we to believe that if a child joins the armed forces then somewhere along the way we have failed? Do we think the curriculum needs to be re-evaluated because one of our students chose the military?

Washington Post reporter Lisa Rein wrote about the resentment many are feeling with President Obama's push to place more veterans into federal employment. With veterans moving to the front of the hiring queue in the biggest numbers in a generation, there's growing bitterness on both sides, according to dozens of interviews with federal employees. Rein went on to report that those who did not serve in the military bristle at times at the preferential hiring of veterans and accuse them of a blind deference to authority. Veterans chafe at what they say is a condescending view of their skills and experience and accuse many non-veterans of lacking a work ethic and sense of mission.

Veterans are not looking for a handout. They understand the value of hard work, of not being rewarded for just participating. They just want to be treated the same as everyone else and not isolated from a society that does not understand what they have gone through.

Everyone should remember that freedom has a cost and our military is our defense against foreign aggression. We must also remember that the great nations of the past have collapsed into tyranny and oblivion because of internal decay and almost never from external forces. There will always be those seeking power and control and they must be identified and eliminated from government. It is the joint responsibility of the military and the civilian population to prevent this degeneration through responsible behavior when possible, and force when necessary. At all costs, the military should never become just the brutal tool of a tyrannical government used to control the population and wage foreign wars to enhance the financial and political interests of despotic rulers. Part of the solution is the mutual respect and support between our armed forces and our civilian population. Those who try to drive a wedge between the two have evil designs on both groups.

SECTION SEVEN:
ISOLATION OF THE SHEEP DOG

The willingness with which our young people are likely to serve in any war, no matter how justified, shall be directly proportional to how they perceive the veterans of earlier wars were treated and appreciated by their nation. These words were penned by George Washington.

The US Code 38 USC-101 defines a veteran as "a person who served in the active military, naval or air service and who was discharged or released therefrom under conditions other than dishonorable." For the purpose of this report, a veteran is defined as "anyone who has served on active duty in any job capacity while a member of the Army, Navy, Air Force, Marines, Coast Guard active components, or of the National Guard or reserves, regardless of discharge status."

On December 8, 2011 The Pew Research Center issued an article called "The Difficult Transition from Military to Civilian Life," in which they said, "Military service is difficult, demanding, and dangerous, but returning to civilian life also poses challenges for the men and women who have served in the armed forces." According to a recent survey of 1,853 veterans done by the organization, more than 7 in 10 veterans (72%) reported that they had an easy time readjusting to civilian life. Twenty-seven percent said re-adjusting was difficult for them—a proportion that swells to 42% among veterans who served in the ten years since the September 11th, 2001 terror attacks.

According to the study, veterans who were commissioned officers, and those who had graduated from college were more likely to have an easy time re-adjusting to their post-military life than enlisted personnel and those who were only high school graduates. Veterans who said they had a clear understanding of their missions while they were serving also experienced fewer difficulties transitioning into civilian life than those who did not fully understand their duties or assignments.

In addition, those who served in a combat zone and those who knew someone who was killed or injured also faced steeper odds against an easy re-entry. Veterans who served in the post-9/11 period also reported more difficulties returning to civilian life than those who served in the Vietnam War, Korean War, or WWII eras. (Pew Research 2011)

Where Are the Jobs?

This is the result of America's changing demographics, loss of manufacturing jobs, unpayable government debt, and general incompetence in our government. Veterans who came out of WWII, Korea, or Vietnam were still able to find positions in the blue-collar manufacturing based economy. Those jobs are gone, forced out by high taxation, impossible government restrictions, and other factors associated with a globalized economy. Today, what's left are information and service-based jobs. Veterans returning to civilian life face a shrinking job market, as most of the jobs are already taken. If recent trends continue, the situation will only get worse.

Veterans, who are transitioning and do not have a college degree, will have a harder time adjusting to civilian life if they do not have a marketable skill. All enlisted personnel have at least a high school diploma, but they may not have a college education, and adjustments will have to be made if they are going to integrate back into the U.S. economy. Now add in the additional fact that many veterans who are married with families will face additional responsibilities as they prepare to leave the active forces or are forced out because of the recent draw-down in the Defense Department's budget. Within a depressed economy veterans without a marketable skill or a practical college education (many college degrees these days are useless) are going to find it difficult to obtain meaningful employment. There are a few states where the economy is doing well, and many of the large industrial states such as Illinois, New York, California, and New Jersey are in serious financial trouble.

The Pew Research Center Study of October 5, 2011 titled, "War and Sacrifice In the Post-9/11 Era" reported that 44% of post-9/11 veterans say the re-adjustment to civilian life was difficult. By contrast, just 25% of veterans who served in earlier eras say the same. About half (48%) of all 9/11 veterans say they have experienced strains in family relations since leaving the military. Forty-seven percent say they have had frequent outbursts of anger. One-third (32%) report there have been times when they felt they didn't care about anything.

Only about one half of one percent of the U.S. population has been on active military duty at any given time during the past decade of sustained warfare. Some 84% of post-9/11 veterans say the public does not understand the problems faced by either those in the military or their families. The public agrees, though by a less lopsided majority—71%. This also could be reflective of the fact that the 9/11 veteran is being re-integrated back into civilian life to a society that really doesn't know of their sacrifice. When WWII veterans came home, everybody had sacrificed as a whole. As they moved into their careers or their education, half of all admissions in college or trade schools were veterans. Korea was the same. Vietnam veterans, even though a segment of the society turned on them and blamed them for the conflict in Vietnam, entered the workforce with the WWII generation still part of the US economy. They had an understanding with the WWII veterans and a common background with their own service in Vietnam.

What Happened to the Value of Duty?

Today veterans face a different America! Today's veteran enters the American economy dealing with employers who do not understand what they did. Most employers have never served in the military themselves. So there's a dichotomy of difference between the employer and the veteran. I faced this myself when I left a position in 2007. When I went to job interviews to apply for another position, I was repeatedly asked variants of this question, "I see that you're a reservist. Are you going to deploy?" Although that's not part of what employers are allowed to ask, try proving they are discriminating against you because you were a veteran or a military reservist. Other companies wouldn't even take the chance of hiring me because if they did, I might have to leave and they would be paying the added cost of trying to hire and train somebody else.

All this adds up to the fact that veterans' talents are going to waste and they are not fully integrated or understood as to what they can bring to their new jobs. The Center for a New American Security carried an article by Nancy Burglass and Margaret C. Harnell in April, 2012 which said, "Three factors limit the ability of both federal agencies and community organizations to serve these veterans effectively. First, a cultural gap between civilian and military societies challenges the nation's capacity to care properly for veterans. Fewer than one percent of Americans serve in today's armed forces. So the military frame of reference, while fundamental to the identity of many veterans, is largely foreign to most civilians. Few Americans understand the transformative nature of military service. In many ways this transformation affects veteran wellness. (New American Security 2012)

Second, veteran care faces a leadership gap. Despite their responsibilities to the military community, neither the DOD nor the VA takes responsibility for, oversees, or offers substantial guidance to help address the service-related needs of veterans. One only has to look at the Veterans Affairs scandal this year. How many administrators were held accountable for the lack of treatments of veterans which caused many deaths? Has the Department of Justice investigated the abuse where VA officials fraudulently kept secret lists of patient wait times even as they kept getting bonuses?

Scandal at the VA

Recently Congress passed a $16.3 billion compromise bill which is supposed to address the failings at the VA, and finally fix this troubled agency's provision of veteran care. The only problem is that Washington does what Washington always does with a problem—it spends more money and avoids the responsibility for actually fixing the problem. In this case, instead of just conducting a comprehensive overhaul of the VA, and identifying and solving the problems, the $16.3 billion dollars the government will spend may only serve to perpetuate the situation. Many would be surprised to learn that the majority of personnel who work at the VA are not veterans, including the administrators. Of all the agencies in U.S. government, the VA should be the one agency where the majority of personnel should be veterans.

And finally, there's a gap in services. The Department of Defense largely meets service members' needs. Once they separate from the military, there is no official mechanism to transition them to the care of another organization such as the VA or another appropriate community-based organization. (New American Security 2012) The computer database for both the Defense Department and Veterans Affairs are not linked together; this should be a wake-up call to all concerned, especially Washington!

Before I left active duty, I attended the Transition Assistance Program. I was given a lot of good information, and I was given information about certain areas of education—vocational, employment, or entrepreneurial. But once I left the TAP program, after one full week of training, there was no follow-up. There was nobody to transition me to another agency. I was pretty much told, "Here's the information. Good luck. Have a nice life." So there is no transition into what happens once a veteran reaches the civilian community. It's wasting valuable veteran talent that could be better utilized, but also, in terms most taxpayers can understand, it's wasting boatloads of taxpayer money.

Tax Dollars Wasted

An article by Arthur S. D. Groat at Kansas State University titled, "Looking Critically At Re-Integration of Post-9/11 Era Military Veterans" said the following: "The Department of Defense is required by statute to fund the unemployment insurance for its recent out-of-work veterans. A senior Pentagon official recently reported the cost that the military services paid for roughly 250,000 people to be approximately $750 million per year with the Army bearing the largest burden. While legitimate disability costs are unavoidable, unemployment is something that can be mitigated.

Groat also notes that third major economic cost to bear is that of educating our veterans in transition. Despite a $42.2 million social investment, current statistics indicate that the post-9/11 GI bill is not fulfilling its political and social promise to infuse our stagnant economy with 2.3 million productive veteran workers, entrepreneurs, and small business start-ups.

There's a lack of effort to re-integrate returning veterans who are different demographically than in prior conflicts. One of the greatest demographics is women. There are more women serving in the military and in more combat roles than at any time in history. There are changing demographics confronting veterans that haven't existed in previous wars and these issues need to be addressed.

Texas Promotes Veterans

Texas has a program called Mission of Momentum Texas, Inc., which has four main missions:

1. Promote motivated economic growth and community development practices throughout Texas.

2. Promote successful business development and job creation in low and moderate income areas throughout Texas.

3. Promote successful business development through female-owned and minority-owned businesses.

4. Assist in the development and financing of affordable housing and neighborhood community facilities.

Many of the most successful programs are at the state and local levels, including numerous non-profit groups. There is no national strategy to integrate the vast number of federal agencies and departments and to also include the states in a coordinated effort to reintegrate veterans back into civilian society. There has been no audit of how successful these various programs are at re-integrating returning veterans. We all want to help veterans adjust to civilian life, but we still have to remember the Department of Veterans Affairs is a government program which has all the trappings of bloated budgets and government mismanagement.

For myself, as an entrepreneur, I started my own business, but there was no guidance on how to start it. When I went through the TAP program, they taught you a little bit about what you need to start a business. They brought someone in who has owned a business and who can provide information to you in case you wanted to own your own business.

There is nothing that teaches you how to write a business plan or how to execute all of its elements. You are instructed about the various licensing you will need, but then what do you do next? There is no follow through after you leave the transition classes. It would be better if each state, in conjunction with the federal government, could coordinate services provided to the veterans in that state.

Small Business Administration

The Small Business Administration (SBA) has numerous programs for veterans including learning about being an entrepreneur, but how successful are these programs? I never found any value in them. The best help I found was my business mentor whom I found by happenstance at a business group I joined in Florida.

Every other government program seemed to be just a colossal waste of time and money.

I learned most of what I know from my mentor about how to brand my business, how to market it, how to utilize public relations in order or to expand my business, how to finance it, how to effectively organize the business, and how to execute product management of my business. As I've said earlier, I made numerous mistakes over time, but my new team has done a great job of integrating the expertise they have to help me become more grounded and more structured regarding where I need to go. There's a lot of wasted veteran talent that could and should be better utilized by veterans who are beginning their new careers as entrepreneurs.

Veterans can be great entrepreneurs; they have the skills in many fields that are needed in American business. Texas is very big in the natural gas and oil industry and many veterans are going into this field where the pay is excellent and there are great benefits. Not every veteran has the ability to do sophisticated mathematics, research, and cutting edge development, but those very few who do should be considered national assets and educated and employed accordingly. On the other hand—and this is very important, veterans must not be intimidated by those with college degrees. Except for degrees in subjects like engineering, physics, mathematics and computer science, many of today's college educations are yesterday's high school educations. This is not an exaggeration. Not everything has to be done on a collegiate or a scholastic level. There are many trade and vocational positions to be had; unfortunately economic policies by various states and the federal government are hindering economic growth. Veterans already have the training they need and they could be integrated into these programs quickly and with minimal cost. As a nation we need to look at how we are spending our money. We should spend it wisely and partner up with state, local, non-profit, and religious organizations to make sure we integrate our veterans into American society. Too often the veteran just falls off. Everybody supports vets until the bands fade away and the adulation fades. The veteran is then stuck without the needed support.

There are additional government-created obstacles for veterans (and other Americans) being accepted for graduate school. One is "affirmative action" (discrimination) which mandates racial and gender quotas over demonstrated ability for admission. Another is a preference for foreign students. A review of authors of scientific papers or college enrollments will verify this. A friend's son was homeschooled (by his widower father) and was accepted to college. Because of his entrance grades he skipped the first year or so of college, graduated, and entered graduate school. Soon thereafter he was asked to teach undergraduate classes. He said he would, but asked if that wasn't normally done by advanced graduate students. He was told that it was normally done that way, but none of the advanced graduate students could speak English well enough to teach.

Veterans have unique attributes, but they also face some unique challenges. One of them is that many veterans are coming out of the military married and that adds financial and sometimes personal stress. They are also entering a society that doesn't really understand what a veteran accomplished and what a veteran can do to impact a business. A strong mentor program, like Momentum Texas accomplishes a valuable service, integrating veterans with mentors in all phases in the different metropolitan areas of a state where there are high concentrations of veterans. This type of a model program should be looked at and adjusted to fit the needs of veterans in each state to make sure they are fully integrated back into American society.

SECTION EIGHT:
CHALLENGES FACING AMERICA'S SAVIORS

Veterans from all conflicts face challenges when they reintegrate back into society and begin to chart new paths after their military service is completed. Veterans of the conflicts in Iraq and Afghanistan are no different, except these veterans are returning to a country tired of war, and in which it was only the military who had sacrificed after September 11th. The U.S. public really had no connection to the conflicts, except when they viewed the images television newscasts or listened to policy debates. These two conflicts never impacted the lives of ordinary Americans as so many other conflicts had throughout American history.

Veterans from all conflicts faced challenges reintegrating back into the fabric of American society. The veterans of 9/11 also face challenges; for many, it is the daunting and well-publicized complications of mental health and disability.

The "Stigma" of PTSD

Far too often veterans are associated by the media with the stigma of having mental health problems. Many people believe all veterans have some form of post-traumatic stress disorder, commonly known as PTSD. What is not publicized is the widespread overmedication of veterans. Many suspect that this is a cheap substitute for more effective but expensive treatment.

An opinion piece appeared in the *Portland Press Herald* on April 8, 2014 and the editors of the paper commented that, "PTSD is a big concern for most veterans, but the whole story is more complex. A 2012 report on veterans' unemployment surveyed nearly 70 companies from all sectors on questions and barriers regarding veterans in the workforce. A majority of companies surveyed said that negative stereotypes, including but not limited to, perceptions of pervasive Post-Traumatic Stress were a major factor in decisions not to hire veterans."

The *Herald* continued, "Many of our veterans feel ambivalent about our wars and alienated from society upon coming home. A large number of Iraq veterans struggled to find a place in civilian society whether in the workforce or elsewhere."

This may be hard to believe in a country that publicly venerates its returning veterans as heroes when given the chance, offering standing ovations at baseball games, and applause in airports, "I support our troops" bumper stickers, flag waving, Budweiser® commercials, and a sea of goodwill from charitable groups.

All veterans have experienced this sort of adulation coming from the public, and veterans appreciate the support, especially the encouragement offered from Vietnam veterans who wanted to ensure we did not face the same homecoming trauma and alienation they had experienced.

Don't be confused though. Those gestures, while doubtlessly heartfelt, do very little to bridge the yawning divide between the military and the civilian worlds in an age when vast swaths of the country simply don't know anyone who serves." They also do not mean that those doing the applauding actually want to know what troops went through or are willing to avoid jumping to the conclusions that an unhinged soldier must have been unhinged because he was a veteran of our two longest wars.

Left unchallenged, the potential popular conception of the veteran as a loose cannon can do lasting damage to the community of post-9/11 veterans who are coming home from Afghanistan and Iraq. The vast majorities of Iraq veterans (including those with Post Traumatic Stress Disorder) come home and leave the service without incident and re-integrate into their communities. This transition is not always easy and is often made more difficult by misperceptions within civilian society about military service and combat stress.

Broken Man Syndrome

Too often society has a negative view of returning veterans, but can you blame them when the media almost always portrays veterans as physically injured and in most cases mentally impaired. Even organizations catering to returning veterans, whether disabled or not, constantly run advertisements soliciting funding for the various programs, that can also reinforce the stigma that all veterans have some type of mental or physical aliment, and businesses do not want to deal with the challenges veterans face.

The vast amount of coverage by the media reporting on the Fort Hood shooting in April of 2014, perpetrated by Iraq war veteran Ivan Lopez makes the transition harder for the millions of Iraq and Afghanistan veterans who will now encounter a public led to believe that all post-9/11 veterans are powder kegs. (Carter 2014)

One Marine that I meet at a transition class related that a potential employer wondered if he should worry about the Marine's mental stability and if he would be more prone to committing a violent act in the workplace.

On April 9, 2013, an article titled "Recent War Vets Face Hiring Obstacles, PTSD Bias" appeared in *USA Today*. The article mentioned that military leaders and veteran advocates worry about hidden hiring discrimination against Iraq and Afghanistan war vets by employers who see the veterans, perhaps, as emotionally damaged.

A key concern is that this could be contributing to the stubbornly high joblessness among the veterans who volunteered to serve in the military after the 9/11 attacks. Because employers are barred by law from asking job applicants about mental health conditions many assume that any veteran can be afflicted with post-traumatic stress disorder (PTSD), although the vast majority return from war without emotional problems," Research and Veteran Advocates, (Zoroya 2013)

A research report from the Center for New American Security, a Washington, DC based think-tank, summarized the finding of interviews with executives of 69 leading corporations, including Bank of America, Target, Walmart, Proctor & Gamble, and Raytheon. All said hiring veterans can be good business, but more than half acknowledged harboring a negative image of veterans because of how popular media, from news coverage to films, portrayed PTSD. (Harrell & Berglass 2012)

Over-Medication of Veterans

Government and private researchers estimate that PTSD is present in 5-20% of the 1.6 million veterans who've served since 9/11. The Department of Veterans' Affairs, which has treated about 56% of those veterans, reports 117,000 diagnosed cases. On May 14, 2014, CBS News reported on an article titled "VA's Over-Medication of Vets Widespread", from the U.S. Inspector General's office . "A federal investigation confirmed Wednesday what CBS News reported on last year. That many wounded veterans are now being over-medicated in VA hospitals. Some overdoses have been fatal. The Inspector General and the Department of Veterans' Affairs discovered the problem is widespread."

CBS News had previously reported on September 19, 2013 in another piece titled, "Veterans Dying from Over-Medication" in which the network reported findings that veterans by the tens of thousands have come home from Iraq and Afghanistan with injuries suffered on the battlefield. Many of them seek treatment at veteran's hospitals.

This phenomenon has greatly impacted the veteran community! Many veterans know the destructive nature of over-medication which has impacted the lives and families of far too many veterans. One Marine I know was diagnosed with a mental disorder, but the medical establishment in the military kept giving him numerous anti-depression medications, and the side effects eventually led to his death.

Yet another CBS News investigation has found that some veterans are dying of accidental overdoses of narcotic painkillers at a much higher rate than the general population. Some of the VA doctors are speaking out. CBS News obtained VA data through a records request that shows the number of prescriptions written by VA doctors and nurse practitioners during the past 11 years. The number of patients treated by the VA is up 29% but narcotics prescriptions are up 259%." (Axelrod 2013)

Suicides in the Military

The issue of the high number of suicides impacting the armed forces has many believing this is directly related to the over-medicating of veterans. While on active duty I witnessed firsthand many Marines returning after seeking treatment for mental health related issues, and in each instance they also returned with substantial amounts of prescription related anti-depressant medication. Studies are needed to analyze the effect of the different medications and their effects on veterans. Too often alcohol was a contributing factor in many of the suicides in combination with excessive use of prescription anti-depression medications. Veterans seeking or forced to seek mental health treatment are already depressed; many have alcohol related issues along with their depression which have not been properly dealt with. Under these conditions additional anti-depression medication can place them at risk for committing suicide. This may all be done without proper supervision and or monitoring to analyze how they are coping. This is also prevalent in many Reserve and National Guard Forces who are often released from active duty without the proper care or supervision needed to ensure they are being treated appropriately.

Now all the blame should not be attributed to the Department of Veterans Affairs, or various military medical personnel. The armed forces and military commanders have not done enough in handling and ensuring their personnel receive the treatment and care they need. This is something I experienced firsthand where Marines exhibiting mental or health related symptoms were transferred from their parent command to other units, as it was far easier for units to just move the personnel around without having to deal with the effects of mental health among their Marines. Far too often military commanders found it easier to send personnel exhibiting mental health or other related issues somewhere else than be forced to confront the challenges they faced, and in many instances the way to deal with the problem was with some sort of administrative separation.

How many military personnel were administratively separated from service after having served in Iraq and Afghanistan because they had exhibited signs of mental health issues, and usually after some offense had been committed? These veterans may still receive treatment through the VA, but with an administrative discharge which usually has the stigma of a less than honorable discharge. Employment forms have boxes for service in the military and conditions of discharge. When the veteran checks "yes"—he served and "no"—he was not honorably discharged he has to explain this situation. The employer will then most likely send the application to the recycling file. As employers who have never served know, a discharge of less than honorable means that something happened negatively and the employer will not take a chance and the veteran will probably not be offered employment. Because of this, the veteran may be excluded from most or all the jobs for which he applies. Sooner or later he may join the ranks of homeless Iraq/Afghanistan veterans living on the streets with no resources and no hope of employment.

VA Crisis Escalates

In its written testimony for a congressional hearing, The American Legion presented two key points from an online survey it conducted on veterans who suffer from traumatic brain injury (TBI) and post-traumatic stress disorder (PTSD):

- Medication appears to be the Department of Veterans Affairs front-line treatment reported by respondents

- A sizeable proportion of respondents reported prescriptions of up to 10 medications for PTSD/TBI across their treatment experiences. (Callaghan 2014)

Medical Daily ran an article in its November 12, 2013 edition entitled "Veterans Administration Accused of Over-medicating War Veterans" with the following subtitle "Many now battling addictions along with pain." It stated, "Accused of over-medicating soldiers returning from the war, the US Veterans Administration (VA) has been directed by Congress to re-assess how doctors prescribe dangerously addictive painkillers."

A report released in September of 2012 by the Center for Investigative Reporting (CIR) as part of data obtained utilizing the Freedom of Information Act reported that since the 9/11 terrorist attacks, the agency charged with helping veterans recover from war instead masks their pain with potent drugs, feeding addictions, and contributing to a fatal overdose rate among VA patients that is nearly double the national average.

Prescriptions for four opiates—hydrocodone, oxycodone, methadone, and morphine—have surged by 270 percent in the past 12 years, according to data CIR obtained through the Freedom of Information Act. CIR's analysis for the first time exposes the full scope of that increase, which far outpaced the growth in VA patients and varied dramatically across the nation. (Glantz 2013)

The agency has long been aware of the problem. In 2009, new VA regulations required clinicians to follow an "integrated approach" to helping veterans in pain, including a stronger focus on treating the root causes of pain rather than using powerful narcotics to reduce symptoms.

But despite the regulations, VA doctors appear to be prescribing more opiates than ever and the data suggests that adoption of the regulations varies wildly.

Given the recent scandal at the Department of Veterans Affairs, there has never been a better time to do a top-to-bottom review of all aspects of how veteran care is being administered. Too often Washington's answer to problems is to allocate additional funding resources, but often funding is not the correct solution. Suicides have wreaked havoc across the armed forces, but has anyone completed a comprehensive and though examination of the effects of over-medication and suicides? We become outraged, and rightfully so, at the scourge of suicides rampant across the armed forces.

Washington Fails to Act

Congress has oversight ability over the Department of Veterans Affairs, and with the recent scandal at the VA has Congress thoroughly investigated the overmedication of veterans and its potential impact on military suicides? Will congress be outraged or will the outrage be because it's an election year and they want to show their constituents they are taking care of veterans? Many elected officials become outraged but always seem to place it in the guise of partisan politics without ever addressing the root cause of the problem.

A national study found that veterans of Iraq and Afghanistan with mental health diagnoses, particularly PTSD, are significantly more likely than veterans with no mental health diagnoses to receive prescription opioid medications for pain-related conditions. The association between PTSD and opioid prescription was statistically strong because it was significant for all subgroups of veterans with PTSD. Moreover, veterans with other mental disorders (e.g., substance use disorders and traumatic brain injury) were more likely to receive prescription opioids when PTSD was present as a comorbid diagnosis. Veterans with mental health diagnoses prescribed opioids, especially those with PTSD, were more likely to have comorbid drug and alcohol use disorders; receive higher-dose opioid regimens, continue taking opioids longer, receive concurrent prescriptions for opioids, sedative hypnotics, or both, and obtain early opioid refills. Finally, receiving prescription opioids was associated with increased risk of adverse clinical outcomes for all veterans returning from Iraq and Afghanistan, especially for veterans with PTSD who were at highest risk of alcohol, drug, and opioid related accidents and overdose, as well as self-inflicted injuries. (Kar 12)

Senators Susan Collins (R-ME) and Richard Blumenthal (D-CT) introduced a bipartisan bill, co-sponsored by Senators Barbara Boxer (D-CA), Joe Manchin (D-WV), Lisa Murkowski (R-AK), and John Boozman (R-AR), that seeks to address the issue of prescription drug abuse among our nation's service members and veterans. The Service members and Veterans Prescription Drug Safety Act would direct the Attorney General to establish drug take-back programs in coordination with the Department of Defense (DOD) and the Department of Veterans Affairs (VA). A bill was introduced, but who is actually looking into this problem? The VA scandal should be a perfect opportunity to conduct a comprehensive overhaul of how the VA implements the medical treatment of veterans. So far it seems to be just another government study with no real impact on the lives of veterans, when an independent investigation outside of the government apparatus is sorely needed.

Astoundingly, the number of reported suicide deaths among service members reached 349 in 2012. Moreover, according to data collected by the Department of Veterans Affairs from 21 states, 22 veterans take their own lives each day. (Collins 2013)

"America lost more veterans to suicide than we did in Afghanistan last year—65% involving the use of drugs—which is a preventable epidemic we must take every action possible to counter," said Senator Murkowski. "The VA has acknowledged that overmedicating our veterans is doing them a disservice by not allowing them to fully heal and can lead to counterproductive, depressed thoughts and behaviors. Giving our men and women in uniform an avenue to return unneeded and dangerous drugs removes a threat from their own medicine cabinets," Sen. Murkowski concluded.

Who has been held accountable for the over-medicating of our veterans? Has anyone detailed a comprehensive study with recommendations that will ensure our veterans are not having their lives and families ruined because of over medication? What about our Reserve and National Guard personnel who often are sent back home without the full resources active duty personnel have access to.

"Many of our veterans struggle with dependencies on prescription drugs. Drug take-back programs designed specifically for service members offer a safe option to dispose of old or unneeded medications to help reduce the risk of developing addictions to prescription drugs," Senator Boozman said. "This legislation is a common sense tool that will help reduce the misuse of medications for those who serve in uniform." (Collins 2013)

With all the focus on the Veterans Affairs scandal, now is the time for a comprehensive and detailed analysis of the treatment of veterans at the VA and throughout the Department of Defense. This has to include veterans with mental health related issues and how these issues affect veterans and their families.

Paid Not To Work

National Affairs, Issue No. 16 of the Summer of 2013, published an article, "A Better Way to Help Veterans," in which the authors wrote, "A shocking 45% of veterans from the wars in Iraq and Afghanistan are currently seeking compensation for service-connected disabilities. That's more than twice the application rate of troops who served in the Gulf War. There are many reasons for this increase, but a major factor is surely the design of VA benefit policies which distort incentives and encourage veterans to live off government support instead of working to their full capability. Adding to the problem is a culture of low expectations fostered by the misguided understanding of disability upon which both federal policy and private philanthropy are often based. The result is that for many veterans a state of dependency that should be temporary instead becomes permanent." (Gade 2013)

The definition of "disability" in the VA system is such that most of these veterans are not disabled in the way that most Americans understand the term. It would be far more accurate to describe these veterans as simply having a service-connected condition."

Assessing the true prevalence of PTSD can be difficult. The task has become even more complicated by two changes to VA policies in 2010 regarding diagnosis and treatment. First, the VA no longer requires proof that the veteran actually experienced a specific traumatic experience because PTSD can rise from an accumulation of stress, particularly the persistent fear of enemy or terrorist activity that characterizes service in a combat zone. Second, rather than simply observing PTSD in the patients who come to a clinic seeking treatment, the VA now actively pursues patients who might have the condition using public awareness campaigns such as "PTSD Awareness Month" in June. One result of the changes is that more veterans with legitimate diagnoses of PTSD are receiving the treatment they need. Another is that the claims for PTSD-related benefits and the figures for veteran disability have sky-rocketed. Among Iraq and Afghan veterans the Department of Veterans Affairs reported 261,998 cases of diagnosed PTSD as of the first quarter of 2013—a prevalence much greater than amongst previous generations of combat veterans.

The Department of Veterans Affairs is also making it easier to qualify for benefits on the basis of Traumatic Brain Injury or TBI. In December, 2012, the agency unveiled new regulations that would allow thousands of veterans to receive benefits for five diseases not previously covered by the VA, basing the expansion on a 2008 Institute of Medicine study that found "limited or suggestive" evidence that these diseases might sometimes be linked to TBI. Incidentally, only a small fraction of the 250,000 cases of TBI diagnosed among service members since 2000 are combat related. The vast majority stem from vehicle crashes, training incidents, or sports injuries.

The most troubling aspect is that many non-veterans see veterans as potential victims with the pendulum swinging to over-compensating for any perceived misfortune remotely related to government service. The point I am making is that there are veterans who legitimately need benefits associated with their military service, and they should receive those benefits in a timely manner. I want to ensure that those who earned their benefits are receiving the benefits and care associated with their injuries, and that the VA system is not being overwhelmed by those who are simply after compensation.

Victimization

Contrary to some conventional opinions, most veterans are not "victims" or members of a problem class. Given their educational and health advantages, those returning from the wars in Iraq and Afghanistan are likely to be a particularly valuable asset to America's economy and society in the years ahead. It is therefore important, from a purely economic point of view, to ensure that as many of them as possible are working to their full capacity. This means targeting assistance to those veterans who are genuinely struggling with the transition back to civilian life, while avoiding giving more capable veterans reason to work below their potential (or to not work at all). From a moral point of view, the argument for veteran's full re-integration through employment is even stronger. (Gade 2013)

Veterans are not victims as portrayed by society. This may be part of the dichotomy and the mind set of many Americans, but not from veterans. We do not want charity, pity, or anything else associated with being a victim. We just want to be treated like everyone else. Let us show this nation what veterans are capable of, let us lead like we lead on the battlefield. The World War II generation transformed America and this new generation of Americans can again transform our country.

The June 2, 2014 issue of *The Weekly Standard* on, quoted Mackubin Thomas Owens in an article titled "Combating the Veteran as a Victim Narrative," in which he wrote, "The highly regarded and greatly admired former Commander of U.S. Central Command, retired Marine General James Mattis argued in a recent speech to veterans of the wars in Iraq and Afghanistan, 'Those Americans are wrong. You've been told that you're broken,' said Mattis during a Q & A portion of his April 23rd speech at the Marine Memorial Club in San Francisco, 'That you're damaged goods and should be labeled the victims of two unjust and poorly executed wars. I don't buy it. The truth instead is that you are the only folks with the skills, determination, and values to ensure American dominance in this chaotic world. There is no room for military people, including our veterans, to see themselves as victims even if so many of our countrymen are prone to relish that role.' He continued, 'While "victimhood" in America is exalted, I don't think our veterans should join those ranks.'"(Owens 2014)

While not denying the existence of PTSD, General Mattis offers an alternative that he calls Post-Traumatic Growth. Post-Traumatic Growth (PTG) has echoes of Nietzsche's aphorism from *Twilight of the Idols,* "From life's goal of war, what does not kill me makes me stronger." In Mattis' view, PTG describes the fact that most veterans return from war with the potential to be stronger than before. The PTG orientation holds that what the returning veteran needs is the time and support to actualize the potential for growth. (Owens 2014)

Veterans need time to reintegrate back into society. The veterans returning from World War II were given the time they needed to adjust to post-military life. As they were returning from Europe and the Pacific battlefields, because transportation home took weeks instead of hours, they were able to relive their experiences with other veterans who experienced the same situations before they were discharged from the military. The economy for the returning veterans was vastly different than is the case today. Today's veterans are rightfully concerned about being released back into the declining American economy where there are already too few jobs available, governments at all levels are functionally bankrupt, and our political "leaders" seem intent on leading the country into oblivion.

Alienation at Home

The speech Lieutenant General Kelly gave was mentioned previously but it also pertains to the alienation of veterans and is worth repeating. On November 13, 2010, Lieutenant General John Kelly addressed the Semper Fi Society of St. Louis just days after learning his son had been killed in Afghanistan, "Most wearing the eagle, globe, and anchor today join the unbroken ranks of heroes after that fateful day, not for money or promises of bonuses or travel to exotic liberty ports, but for one reason, and one reason alone, because of the terrible assault on our way of life by men they knew must be killed and an extremist ideology that must be destroyed. A plastic flag in their car window was not their response to the murderous assault on our country. No, their response was a commitment to protect the nation—swearing an oath to their God to do so to their deaths. When future generations ask why America is still free in the hey-day of al Qaeda and was counted in days rather than in centuries, as the extremists themselves predicted, our hometown heroes (soldiers, sailors, airmen, coast guards, and the Marines) can say, "Because me and people like me risked all to protect millions who will never know my name." (Fraser 2010)

Lieutenant General Kelly continued, "American civilian and military protectors, both here at home and overseas, have for nearly nine years fought this enemy to a standstill and have never for a second wondered why. They know and are not afraid. Their struggle is your struggle. They hold in disdain those who claim to support them but not the cause that takes their innocence, their limbs and even their lives. As a democracy, we the people, and by that definition is every one of us, sent them away from home and hearth to fight our enemies. We are all responsible. I know it doesn't apply to those of here tonight. But if anyone thinks you can somehow thank them for their service and not support the cause for which they fight—America's survival—then they are lying to themselves and rationalizing away something in their lives. But, more importantly, they are slighting our warriors and mocking their commitment to the nation." (Fraser 2010)

Lieutenant General Kelly made one bold statement, "It is a fact that our country today is in a life-and-death struggle against an evil enemy. But America, as a whole, is certainly not at war. Not as a country; not as a people. Today only a tiny fraction (less than 1%) shoulders the burden of fear and sacrifice and they shoulder it for the rest of us. Their sons and daughters who serve are men and women of character who continue to believe in this country enough to put life and limb on the line without qualification and without thought of personal gain. They serve so that the sons and daughters of the other 99% don't have to. No big deal though, as Marines have always been the first to fight—paying in full the full bill that comes with being free for everyone else." (Fraser 2010)

Again, here is another statement that was mentioned previously, but is very applicable to how veterans feel society treats them. Colonel Peter Mansoor wrote a book called *Baghdad at Sunrise*. "Fifteen months after my return from Iraq, I was invited to a cocktail reception on the Upper East Side of Manhattan. After discovering that the son of the host and hostess was interested in military affairs, I suggested that, since the US Military Academy was just up-river from New York City, perhaps he should consider applying for admission.

"The hostess blanched, put her arm around her son's shoulder and replied, 'No, no, no. He has much more important things planned for his life.' She then patted me on the arm and said, 'But I'm glad we have people like you, people to protect us.' " (Mansoor 2008)

In his book, *On Combat,* Lieutenant Colonel Dave Grossman writes, "One Vietnam veteran—an old, retired colonel—once said to me, 'Most people in our society are sheep. They are kind, gentle, productive creatures who only hurt one another by accident. I mean nothing negative by calling them sheep. To me it's like the pretty blue robin's egg. Inside its soft and gooey, but some day it will grow into something wonderful, but the egg can't survive without its hard blue shell. Police officers, soldiers, and other warriors are like that shell. Someday the civilization they protect will grow into something wonderful. For now though, they need warriors to protect them from the predators."

Grossman continued: "Then there are wolves," the old war veteran said. "The wolves feed on the sheep without mercy. Do you believe there are wolves out there who will feed on the flock without mercy? You better believe it. There are evil men in this world and they are capable of evil deeds. The moment that you forget that or pretend it is not so, you become a sheep. There is no safety in denial.

"Then there are sheepdogs," he went on, "And I'm a sheepdog. I live to protect the flock and confront the wolf. Or as a sign in one California law enforcement agency put it, "We intimidate those who intimidate others." If you have no capacity for violence then you are a healthy productive citizen—a sheep. If you have a capacity for violence and no empathy for your fellow citizens then you have defined yourself as an aggressive psychopath, a wolf. But what if you have a capacity for violence and deep love for your fellow citizen? Then you are a sheepdog. A warrior is someone who is walking the hero's path, someone who can walk into the heart of darkness, into the universal human phobia, and walk out unscathed.

"Let me expand on this old soldier's excellent model of the sheep, wolves and sheepdogs," Grossman said. "We know that the sheep live in denial; that is what makes them sheep. They do not want to believe that there's evil in the world. They can accept the fact that the fires can happen which is why they want fire extinguishers, fire sprinklers, fire alarms and fire exits throughout their kids' schools. But many of them are outraged at the idea of putting an armed police officer in their kids' school. Our children are dozens of times more likely to be killed and thousands of times more likely to be seriously injured by school violence than by school fires. The sheep's only response to the possibility of violence is denial. The idea of someone coming to kill or harm their children is just too hard so they choose the path of denial.

"The sheep generally do not like the sheepdog. He looks a lot like the wolf; he has fangs and the capacity for violence. The difference though is that the sheepdog must not, cannot and will not ever harm the sheep. Any sheepdog who intentionally harms the lowliest little lamb will be punished and removed. The world can't work any other way, at least, not in a representative democracy or republic such as ours. Still this sheepdog disturbs the sheep. He is a constant reminder that there are wolves in the land. They would prefer that he didn't tell them where to go or give them traffic tickets or stand at the ready in our airports in camouflaged fatigues holding an M-16. The sheep would rather have the sheepdog cash in his fangs, spray paint himself white and go, 'Baaah!' until the wolf shows up. Then the entire flock tries desperately to hide behind one lowly sheepdog. As Kipling said in his poem about Tommy, the British soldier, 'While it's Tommy this and Tommy that and Tommy fall behind, but it's please to walk in front, sir, when there's trouble in the wind. There's trouble in the wind, my boys. There's trouble in the wind. Oh, it's please to walk in front, sir, when there's trouble in the wind.'

"Look what happened after September 11, 2001, when the wolf pounded hard at the door. Remember how America, more than ever before, felt differently about their law enforcement officers and military personnel. Remember how many times you heard the word *hero*. How long did that last? Give credit where it's due. A lot of people stayed alert to the threat and kept their hearts and heads right. But many of them, far too many, quickly forgot. They are sheep. They sink back into denial. They are sheep. They have two speeds: graze and stampede.

"Understand there is nothing morally superior about being a sheepdog. It is just what you chose to be. Also understand that a sheepdog is a funny critter. He's always sniffing around out on the perimeter—checking the breeze, barking at things that go bump in the night and yearning for a righteous battle. That is, the young sheepdogs yearn for a righteous battle.

"The old sheepdogs are a little older and wiser. They move to the sound of the guns when needed right along with the young ones. Here is how the sheep and sheepdog think differently. The sheep pretend the wolf will never come, but the sheepdog lives for that day. After the attacks of September 11, 2001, most of the sheep—that is, most citizens in America—said, 'Thank God I wasn't on one of those planes.' The sheepdogs, the warriors, said, 'Dear God, I wish I could have been in one of those planes. Maybe I could have made a difference.' When you are truly transformed into a warrior and have truly invested yourself into warriorhood, you want to be there. You want to be able to make a difference."

Old Soldiers Never Die; They Just Fade Away

This analogy highlights the veteran of today, everyone supports the veteran, but now the conflict is in the past and we no longer need a strong and viable military to protect—we have other needs. After each conflict America always substantially reduces its armed forces then has to quickly rearm itself to face new challenges. The wolf never seems to go away, but is kept at bay by the sheep dog, but when the sheep dog is alienated by the public or is reviled because he is doing his job, then eventually a pattern is set and few will want to take on the role of the sheepdog.

All pay tribute to veterans but they do not fully understand the contribution veterans have made to this country and will continue to make to ensure our freedom. Veterans will again transform the American landscape in much the same tradition as their World War II counterparts. Just give them the chance.

SECTION NINE:
RESERVE / NATIONAL GUARD

The Reservist

The wars in Iraq and Afghanistan are starting to recede from memory, as the United States has already pulled out of Iraq and will have its remaining forces fully withdrawn from Afghanistan by the end of 2016. Most Reserve and National Guard units have seen a diminished number of re-activations in support of the War on Terror. As we transition from the War on Terror, issues facing reserve and National Guard members are getting less attention than their active duty comrades.

The Congressional Research Service has recently stated, "The term *reserve component* refers collectively to the seven individual reserve components of the armed forces—Army National Guard of the United States, the Army Reserve, Navy Reserve, Marine Corps Reserve, the Air National Guard of the United States, the Air Force Reserve and the Coast Guard Reserve." The purpose of these seven reserve components as codified in law at 10 U.S.C.10102 is to provide training units and qualified persons available for active duty in time of war or national emergency and at such other times as national security may require it to fill the needs of armed forces whenever more units and persons are needed than are in the regular components.

The mobilization of reservists in the aftermath of the September 11, 2001 terrorist attacks has been the largest since the Korean War and one of the longest ongoing mobilizations ever. Some of these reservists have experienced financial losses when moving from their civilian jobs to full-time military status. These losses occur due to differences between the reservists' military and civilian pay, expenses incurred by reservists because of mobilization, and the decline in business experienced by self-employed reservists during and after release from active duty. This has generated numerous complaints from mobilized reservists and helped generate congressional interest in the subject.

Unfortunately as the wars recede into history, issues facing reservists have not gone away. They have just been buried in the morass of Pentagon bureaucracy. Far too often the Department of Defense looks at reserves as second class citizens, because reserves are only to be utilized when the nation needs them, but are summarily cast aside when they are no longer useful. Examples abound on issues facing reserves, from those suffering from PTSD related issues, to employment, and finally personnel facing emotional challenges without the resources afforded their active duty brethren.

The Department of Defense needs to do a comprehensive analysis of all Reserve and National Guard forces and analyze shortfalls and challenges faced by mobilized reserves. The last major call-up of the Reserves was during the first Gulf War, but that was only for a short duration. Before the Gulf War, the last sustained call-up of the Reserves went back to the Korean War. During the Vietnam War, manpower was based only on those who chose to join the military or were drafted into the Armed Forces. The Johnson administration did not want to call up the reserves even though The Joint Chiefs of Staff wanted them to be utilized. Johnson decided against it because of political reasons as he didn't want the mobilization of reserves to have a direct impact on communities across the country.

The nation has relied more heavily on the reserve components since the end of the Cold War. Reservists have been involuntarily activated for federal service six times over the past 23 years. (Kapp 2014)

Some of these activations have been directly related to war or armed conflict. For example, in the Persian Gulf War of 1990-1991, 228,729 reservists were involuntarily activated. In the low intensity conflict with Iraq between the period of 1998-2003, 6,108 reservists were involuntarily activated. In military operations in the aftermath of the September 11 terrorist attack, including operations such as Noble Eagle, Enduring Freedom, and Iraqi Freedom/New Dawn from 2001 to the present, 896,815 reservists were involuntarily or voluntarily activated (as of May 27, 2014). Other activations have been in support of missions that were primarily peace-keeping and nation-building, such as intervention in Haiti (94-96) in which 6,250 reservists were involuntarily activated. In the Bosnian peace-keeping mission (1995-2004), 31,553 reservists were involuntarily activated. For the ongoing Kosovo mission, 11,485 reservists have been involuntarily activated since 2003. The available data since then has listed reservists who have served in a combination of armed conflict and peace-keeping. (Kapp 2014)

Reserve Re-integration

In passing the Operational Reserve Retention and Retirement Reform Congress took the first step in modernizing the reserve retirement system with enactment of early retirement eligibility for certain reservists activated for at least 90 continuous days served since January 28, 2008.

Repeated, extended activations make it more difficult to sustain a full civilian career and impede reservists' ability to build a full civilian retirement, 401(k), etc. Regardless of statutory protections, periodic long-term absences from the civilian workplace often limit Guard/reserve members' upward mobility, employability, and financial security. Further, strengthening the reserve retirement system will serve as an incentive to retaining critical mid-career officers and NCOs for continued service and thereby enhance readiness.

A group known as The Military Coalition which is a consortium of nationally prominent uniformed services and veterans' organizations representing approximately 5.5 million current and former veterans plus their families and survivors testified before a Congressional Subcommittee and made the following recommendations:

- Correct the early retirement credit to include all Guard and reserve members who have served on active duty tours of at least 90 days retroactive to September 11, 2001.

- Modernize the reserve retirement system to reflect the increased service and sacrifice of operational reservists including appropriate credit for active and inactive duty service.

- Allow full-retirement credits for all inactive duty training points earned annually (annual IDT points are capped at 130 presently).

- Correct the Fiscal Year barrier that prevents rollover credit for aggregates of 90 days qualifying active duty served over multiple fiscal years.

- Consolidate the current 30 types of authorities used for orders of Guard-reserve members down to 10 or less. (Senate 2014)

In passing the Yellow Ribbon Reintegration Program Congress has provided increased resources to support the transition of warrior-citizens back into the community. But program execution remains spotty from state to state and falls short for those returning Federal Reserve warriors in widely dispersed regional commands. Programs should meet a standard level of family support within each state. Military and civilian leaders at all levels must improve the coordination and delivery of services for the entire operational reserve force. Many communities are eager to provide support and do it well. But Yellow Ribbon efforts in a number of locations amount to little more than PowerPoint slides but little or no actual implementation. There are programs which assist reservists but again, as for any government program, has anyone looked at their effectiveness?

Additionally, the Military Coalition recommended that the Subcommittee conduct an oversight hearing to review Yellow Ribbon best practices, assess gaps, and take steps to ensure a sustainable program for the operational reserve forces called to active Federal service.

Washington, Where are You?

Despite years of efforts to improve health care and develop support networks for the National Guard and military reserves, these service members report higher rates of mental health problems and related ills than active-duty troops, according to current and former officials, troops, experts, and government studies. This should come as no surprise to anyone in the reserve community, because as soon as you return from deployment you are de-activated and sent home. Unfortunately many Reserve and National Guard personnel live far from any military base, and if they need to seek any sort of treatment related to their activation it usually means taking time off from work which might affect their employment status. Their families are not familiar with the military culture and are rarely trained on the specific problems affecting their recently returned loved ones.

More than 665,000 National Guard and reserve troops—known collectively as the reserve component, have served in Afghanistan and Iraq during the past decade. Upon returning home, many have been hastily channeled through a post-deployment process that has been plagued with difficulties, including a reliance on self-reporting to identify health problems. (Lau 2012)

New research and interviews with those familiar with the military health-care system suggest that attempts by Congress, the military, and private contractors to address the problems have been uncoordinated and often ineffective. From September 2010 to August 2011, post-deployment health-reassessment screenings found that nearly 17 of every 100 returning reservists had mental health problems that were serious enough to require a follow-up. That number is 55 percent greater than active-component service members, according to the Armed Forces Health Surveillance Center. (Lau 2012)

Active -duty troops come home to military bases with free, comprehensive medical care and support networks that help diagnose what military leaders call the signature wounds of the wars that began after the attacks of Sept. 11, 2001, (post-traumatic stress disorder and traumatic brain injury). (Lau 2012) Reserve and National Guard troops are not afforded the same treatment and are often stigmatized by the active component as trying to gain unwarranted compensation.

What programs are set up for reserves? In the last few years reserves were activated, sent to Afghanistan, returned stateside, and then almost immediately de-activated, receiving only the bare minimum of resources. Who follows up with them once they leave active duty? One has to remember many reservists live hours from their home unit or from any major military unit. If they are in need of medical care or have to utilize the Veterans Affairs system, it's on their own time and the reservist has to take time off from work. Why again would anyone want to hire a reservist?

Reservists do not have access to the same system or networks that experts say are needed to assess and treat their injuries. After brief demobilization assessments, reserve troops return home and must navigate disparate health-care and support providers, often without the psychological safety net that comes from living near members of their unit. (Lau 2012)

Those who are reading this book need to understand that there is a difference between voluntary activation and involuntarily activation. The latter means the government calls you, you're not volunteering. Voluntary activation is when you voluntarily choose to meet a mission that the armed forces are involved in. You voluntarily decided to go on active duty. There are two big distinctions between voluntary and involuntary activation and the difference has many legal ramifications, especially when it comes to keeping your employment.

The Missing Link

As for reservists—and this is where I fell in because I've been in reserve most of my life except for a short period of three or four years when I was on active duty in my initial enlistment in the Marines. I had volunteered for activation right after 9/11, but I was involuntarily activated as part of the orders.

When I deployed or got activated my first time, I was on active duty for two years. I did a tour of duty in Afghanistan and came back. I was back at the base at Camp Pendleton where I had various assignments. I was stop-lossed (a military term for an involuntary extension of duty) because they needed military personnel to be part of the conflict in Iraq. The differences between the active and the reserve component is that in the active duty, when you come back from a conflict like in Iraq or Afghanistan, you go right back into your military job at whatever base you came from. Reserves would come back and could stay on just until they settled in before going home.

As the war lingered on, especially around 2009 or 2010, the military quickly processed you out back to your civilian jobs. The biggest issues that reserves were facing depended on what they did in their civilian work. If they worked for the government, their government job was there. If they work in private industry (which a lot of reservists do)—that's not government related—the businesses would have to keep them in the same position. If they were to be promoted, they would take that promotion when they returned. Some of the problems returning soldiers had depended on what company they worked for. If they worked at a major corporation who could absorb the loss of a reservist—it's regrettable that they had to go and it hurt the company, but they could still assimilate fairly easily back into the company and it wasn't a big burden.

Reserve Family Separation

The other aspect not faced from the active duty side is dealing with family arrangements which are different for reservists than for their active duty colleagues. The difference is that almost all active-duty personnel are coming off a base. Their families are at a base, unless they decide to go back home while their spouse is deployed. When reservists are activated, their families reside wherever they were living. Some reservists live near a major military base, but most do not. I was activated from Northern California. I had to go down to Camp Pendleton located in Southern California. I wasn't near my family, and many reservists in my unit lived up in the Los Angeles basin. When reservists activate, some can retain their company health plan, but many have to use the military health plan know as Tri-Care. Some doctors accept it, but if their primary care physician does not, what then? Their family has to find another provider and go through the process of learning the system, so they ask the military member, who probably barely understands how it's to be used. By this time their soldier is deployed and the families have a difficult time reaching him or her, plus the reserve families have minimal access or contact with the service personnel's unit. Even if the soldier stays back in the States, which I did during many periods at this time, they're not near their family. The question becomes, what happens to their family while they deploy?

Reservist; Second Class Citizens

Now, as we go further and further away from the War on Terror, deployments for reserves and National Guard personnel to Iraq and Afghanistan have ended. The issues encountered during the call-up of the reserves and National Guard, haven't been resolved and the Department of Defense needs to restructure the mobilization and deactivation of its National Guard and reserve forces. When we have to go to the next conflict where the reserves and National Guard forces are going to be used heavily, especially with the drawdown of the active duty component, why don't we look at what went right and fix what went wrong instead of repeating the same mistakes? Another issue is that although it's easy to call up reserves and National Guard forces, the transition off of active duty is not well organized. They face additional challenges which are not being addressed. As we came back from Iraq and Afghanistan, reserves and National Guard forces who had medical issues or PTSD resulting from their deployments were rushed through the process and some still faced obstacles even after de-activation. If I had been injured and had to go back to a doctor, there was no major military base nearby, as I lived Northern California. In various regions of the United States reservists and National Guard forces may not be close to a military base, and so they may have to deal with the VA and all the problems associated with it.

Regarding PTSD and mental health issues, if you're back home, your family may not be prepared to help you deal with these problems. The active component lives near a base where they can get local assistance. They have the resources available, but resources aren't usually available for more distant reserve or National Guard soldiers. It's just not there and this problem needs to be addressed.

There are a lot of challenges that the reserves have because they and their families are at a distance from a military base. The real challenge is what happens when they come back. Many of their jobs could be changed. Many of their jobs could be gone.

They're worrying about how they're going to feed their family now because the check stops right when they get off active duty. Active duty, at least, provides a cushion, especially if they retire. At least, if they know that they're going to leave the military service, they have time to prepare, and they have all the resources that can help them. As we move beyond the post-Iraq/Afghanistan era, we really need to start to look at the challenges facing the reserves as we call them up and as we demobilize them, and this includes employment issues. The medical issues and PTSD and all the issues surrounding it need to be re-visited because reserves are very important for the protection of the national security of the United States.

What About the Next Conflict

Too often in the past, once the war was over, we put the reserves back into their regular routine and we don't think of the next conflict until we have to reinvent the whole wheel all over again. I think the American military should be better than that. We just need to have a viable plan and look at these issues as they impact the US military reserve components.

Many small businesses cannot absorb the loss of a reserve or National Guard employee who is activated. I worked for a small consulting firm, and I was able to go to serve my country, but when I got back I had to readjust to my old job. Once I left the consulting firm to go seek other employment, what really hurt me was being a reservist. At the time it was during the height of the surge into Iraq, and a lot of potential employers didn't want to hire me. I remember they were asking me questions like, "I see you're a reservist. Are you going to deploy?" They can't ask you those questions. At the same time, how do I prove that I was being discriminated against because I'm a reservist? There were some companies who wouldn't even offer me a position or have me come in for an interview. Once they saw I was a military reservist, I was denied employment.

When I activated my last time to go to Afghanistan, since I was now a small business owner, I had to close my business down for the duration of my deployment, and then reestablish it once I was deactivated. Before I got off active duty, I went through the Transition Assistance Program (TAP) to really help me re-energize my business. I knew I needed to go in a different direction to make my business more profitable or at least move it in a direction I needed to go. I went to the TAP program and was given some great information. Unfortunately, it was just generic information I already knew, nothing that would give me practical business experience. The TAP business program didn't really teach me a lot of things I needed to know to build a business beyond branding; nothing on the other tangible items I needed to move my business forward.

Once off active duty I was not near a military base where I could routinely seek assistance Reserves and National Guard personnel are on their own.

Once off active duty I decided to seek assistance with a national marketing firm, but they didn't provide me with what I needed to do to move my business forward. They over-promised and under-delivered and I had to go with another marketing team. By this point, it had become a good learning experience because as with any challenge, I came out of it stronger and wiser then when I went into it.

It was by happenstance that I meet the right individual who was a superb coach and a good mentor. He guided me utilizing his 30 years of business experience. He could guide me where I needed to go in each phase from branding to marketing. I thought I was going in one direction when I really needed to go in a different direction. The business became more profitable, and I became more astute about formulating my goals and plans of achieving them. That's why I wanted to eventually set up a group called The Vet Transition Academy. Then I could help other vets learn from the mistakes that I've made and gain from the knowledge that I have on how to move themselves, how to start a business, and also how to find employment.

Let's not wait until the next conflict to address issues and the complex challenges reserves and National Guard forces face with activation. Unfortunately, we always seem to face the problems without learning from past conflicts.

SECTION TEN:
TYPICAL
WASHINGTON!

How many programs are there to reintegrate veterans back into the fabric of U.S. society?

How many millions of dollars does the Department of Defense spend on reintegration programs?

The Department of Veterans Affairs spends additional millions on reintegration programs, but has anyone checked to see how effective these programs are?

The federal government always believes it can spend more money, add another program and solve its problems. Is there any wonder why we are over $17 trillion in debt.

Throughout this book, as I've stated previously, the US government and the Department of Veterans Affairs, Department of Labor, and the Defense Department has spent millions upon millions of dollars (more than a billion dollars in total) to re-integrate veterans. The Department of Defense starts out with its Transition Assistance Program. This program trains veterans before they get out, placing them on an education, employment, or an entrepreneurial track. Once they leave active duty, then they can go to the Department of Veterans Affairs and the Department of Labor for additional assistance. The agencies have additional funding to re-integrate veterans back into society. The only things that are constant is that nobody knows how well these programs work, what's effective, and what's not. The General Accountability Office reported that there are good things that the Department of Defense is doing, but nobody knows how well these programs are working or if they are meeting their intended targets to employ veterans or what their measures of performance and effectiveness are.

The G.I. Bill

There are some things that need to change in order for us to effectively re-integrate veterans. The signature program of the New G.I. Bill which passed in the waning days of the Bush administration, and which was updated in 2009 by President Obama needs to be looked at. Is it meeting its target market? In the closing days of WWII, when the GI Bill passed, it allowed millions upon millions of returning veterans who otherwise wouldn't have had an opportunity to go to college to have the chance to receive a formal education whether through the university system or through a trade program. During this time, half of all students in various educational programs were veterans. How effective is the new G.I. Bill and is it reaching its intended audience? Are there areas where we can make the GI Bill more effective and less bureaucratic for veterans and save the taxpayer money?

Before we start more programs, we need to see what works now and what doesn't. Through various reports, we're seeing that a lot of veterans are not utilizing the new GI bill. So we need to find out why that is the case. Is it because they don't have enough knowledge? Is it because they don't know they qualify? Is the process too cumbersome and filled with bureaucratic hurdles preventing veterans from enrolling? Are veterans utilizing it for vocational training which often pays higher wages? Are institutions scamming veterans over-promising them just to get the federal money associated with it? The Justice Department needs to investigate this to see if any inappropriate behavior is occurring.

There is an additional issue which should be addressed which is a win-win situation for both our veterans and our country. I would like to introduce this with a real-life example. I had a friend who started college with me. I was hard working and motivated, but he wasn't serious enough. He "flunked out", and joined the army. After his hitch in the army, he returned to college, got a PhD in physics, and became a professor. The point here is that, among the large numbers of veterans returning to civilian life there will be some with exceptional talents. It is vital that their capabilities be recognized and they be given special educational opportunities to maximize their talents. These individuals are a desperately needed resource for our country because identifying veterans who possess tremendous potential and equipping them with marketable scientific skills is vital for our survival. Today, when our public educational system is failing and the external threat from foreign commercial and aggressive military competition is greater than ever, it is critical that our outstanding talent be recognized and utilized to maximum effect for their sake and for the sake of our country.

Jedi Knights Across America

From the business side there are a lot of corporate sponsors. GI Jobs listed the 100 most military-friendly companies. So why not partner up with these companies? They provide employment in a wide range of fields including office workers, technicians, and positions requiring all levels of education. Many of them are in interstate commerce, interstate transportation, and oil and gas fields, especially in the North Dakota and Texas areas. Veterans need to know which companies are military-friendly employers because when they apply to these companies being a veteran is one problem they won't have to worry about. There is also a large diversity of job descriptions in their 100 listings.

The other part is partnering up and having different mentors in the different regions that veterans are going to relocate to once they leave active duty. The majority of veterans are coming from just a few states, including California, Texas, Florida and Virginia. Let's look at what those states do and see if it can be duplicated on a national level. Florida's governor and legislature want to make Florida the most military-friendly state in America. If it isn't, that means they consider that they are doing something wrong. Let's look at what Florida's doing and see if that can be duplicated. In Texas, they're doing Momentum Texas where the state does membership/partnership with different corporations. They also do venture capital training and they train entrepreneurs to start their own businesses. Let's look at what Texas is doing to help veterans become entrepreneurs and try to have this duplicated across the country.

When I left active duty, I was left on my own and I decided to go the entrepreneurial route. Beyond just being taught, a veteran has got to get the licenses and know where to go to access services from the different government agencies. It would have been very helpful if I'd had a mentor who could have taken what I had and the idea that I'd had and helped me take it all the way to execution. How do I execute and put together a proper business plan or financial plan? How do I do a comprehensive marketing strategy? How do I do social media? How do I do SEO? I had to learn a lot of that on my own! I made mistakes and I wasted needed capital and time that could have been used for other projects.

Mentoring a Returning Vet

Not every veteran wants to start a business. But why not partner up or mentor veterans in different fields that they want to go into? Some veterans want to go into law enforcement. Maybe let different bases know where there are openings in law enforcement—not just in the state they're from, but throughout the United States. Companies could come to the different military bases and interview for the skills of on-base soldiers who are planning to go into private sector in the near future.

Regarding education, many veterans may be doing 20-30 years or they may just be doing four years of service before leaving the active forces. Let the veterans know of the military-friendly schools in every state. Then they know which schools are available to them that are more military-friendly and will help them integrate successfully. *US Veterans Magazine* maintains a list of the top Military-friendly schools across the country.

Vet Transition Academy

Finally, what I'm establishing in Tampa could be a model to be used all over the US. It could be tweaked to fit the needs of the veteran community in any state. It's called the Vet Transition Academy. It's working with veterans, but not just giving them the information. It's helping them find viable employment by partnering with the business community to employ them and give them the skills needed to reintegrate into the fabric of the U.S. economy.

One example is the mentor who guided me on how to establish a business. He did more than just give me the information to get started, but he looked at my business and assisting me with what I needed and taught me how to execute all aspects in growing my business.

This mentorship was vital to growing my business. Also vital were the introductions to key individuals who would provide guidance in helping with the many questions I had. There were numerous aspects of business development which the TAP program never covered. Social media was never covered in depth, and other aspects were not covered at all.

Government programs, especially the Small Business Administration, gives guidance and assistance, but provides little about how to execute and grow a business.

Veterans can call the Vet Transition Academy at 813-415-3048 to get consultation and guidance on how to reintegrate and how to establish a business.

Gearing Up For Action

We spend billions of dollars trying to facilitate the integration of veterans, but we haven't set the metric to see what works and what doesn't work. We need to work with government agencies, the private sector, corporate America, small businesses, and entrepreneurs. I would even suggest the establishment of an organization which could be led by some of the renowned leaders who've worked with veterans before—two of them being former Secretary of Defense Robert Gates and former Senator James Webb of Virginia who worked with Ronald Reagan as the Secretary of the Navy and was Democratic Senator from Virginia. Let's work with men like those two to set up a national system that we can evaluate to make sure veterans get the resources that they need. Also let's set up a system in which we can help all veterans, including female veterans who have a different focus. They have different concerns which were never considered in the past. We just need to focus on what works. We need to look at what doesn't work and change it so we can re-integrate veterans back into the American society more effectively.

CALL TO ACTION

I have written *The New Business Brigade: Veterans' Dynamic Impact on US Business* because I've had the privilege of serving alongside the finest individuals this nation has produced. Tom Brokaw coined the term "The Greatest Generation" referencing the veterans of World War II; now we are witnessing the "The Next Greatest Generation."

These are the men and women who went off to fight the wars in Iraq and Afghanistan after the tragedy of September 11th. The men and women volunteered to defend this country from the fanatics who wanted to do us harm, with many volunteering time and time again to serve in Iraq and Afghanistan, all to keep the nation safe!

I want the nation, especially the business and political leaders, to know of the brave men and women who dedicated their lives to ensure we enjoy the freedoms we have. You have read this book and have learned about the quality of these individuals and what they can bring to any organization, business, or public service.

There are many challenges facing veterans today, but mainly those challenges come from domestic rather than foreign sources in the form of misinformation which permeates our entertainment industry, our news media, and our political sector. Today's veterans can bring valuable skills to any business with their dedication, experience, and knowledge. They're risk takers. They understand organization, company policy—all these things and more. These are what veterans can bring to an organization. These are the traits veterans can bring to starting a business. You have seen what veterans can do on the battlefield; now watch them succeed here at home.

There are many misconceptions which may cause companies to be reluctant to hire a veteran. As you've read in this book, you can see how those misconceptions are misplaced. I want people across this country to talk about veterans and understand what the veteran can bring. One only has to look back at history to understand what the greatest generation provided this country. They came of age during the Great Depression and served in WWII to provide freedom not only for America, but for mankind. They came back from the cauldrons of war and embraced and reshaped the American landscape and the economy.

All the benefits that we enjoy today are because of what the greatest generation set forth. Now, there's another greatest generation—the generation of Americans who came of age after 9/11. They saw what the terror attacks did to our nation, and they volunteered. They sacrificed; they went off to war in Iraq and Afghanistan. They're serving today. The men and women of the armed forces are the next greatest generation. As those individuals come—as those individuals leave and move on from serving their country in the armed forces, they're going to enter a civilian society that doesn't understand their sacrifice and their tenacity, but, most importantly, the skills that they have. This book has emphasized what these veterans can do to reshape businesses and reshape our country.

As Ronald Reagan once said, "America's greatest days are not behind us. They are ahead of us." As we've seen from this book, these veterans will prove to everybody where they can go. Today the nation's greatest failure could be failing to utilize, failing to understand, but instead marginalizing its veterans to the detriment of this country. Our nation must utilize its veterans. Right now you are reading about the next greatest generation that is going to transform America. Historians in the future will say when America embraced its veterans and utilized those who had come of age during the War on Terror they transformed America and saw that America reached, not for the stars, but for the gates of heaven.

My Inspiration

Two of my favorite speeches are, President John Kennedy's inaugural address in 1961, and President Ronald Reagan's speech commemorating the fortieth anniversary of the D-Day landings at Normandy, France. These two famous addresses symbolize the spirit of America and the character and strength of her armed forces.

President Kennedy stated in his inaugural address, "In the long history of the world, only a few generations have been granted the role of defending freedom in its hour of maximum danger. I do not shrink from this responsibility—I welcome it. I do not believe that any of us would exchange places with any other people or any other generation. The energy, the faith, the devotion which we bring to this endeavor will light our country and all who serve it—and the glow from that fire can truly light the world."

America has never wavered from that responsibility, and members of the armed forces look at themselves as the guardians of freedom, knowing if they falter, the warriors of darkness will be on freedom's doorstep.

President Reagan addressed the world at Pointe du Hoc, France where forty years ago U.S. Army Rangers scaled the cliffs to rescue a suffering humanity. On that windswept day now many years ago, President Reagan declared, "We in America have learned bitter lessons from two World Wars: It is better to be here ready to protect the peace, than to take blind shelter across the sea, rushing to respond only after freedom is lost. We've learned that isolationism never was and never will be an acceptable response to tyrannical governments with expansionist intent."

Now a new threat has emerged, one different than in the past, but one equally as destructive, one who's sole purpose is to expand its reach, and this new threat is Islamic fundamentalism. The horrific event of September 11, 2001, woke the nation to an external threat which seeks to destroy the freedoms we cherish; this scourge seeks to destroy America as it is the one nation which hampers their global ambition.

In his famous inaugural address, President Kennedy stated, "Let every nation know, whether it wishes us well or ill, that we shall pay any price, bear any burden, meet any hardship, support any friend, oppose any foe to assure the survival and the success of liberty."

A new generation of Americans rose up from the ashes and volunteered to confront this new threat without any thought of their own selves, volunteered to go into the breach in Iraq and Afghanistan knowing they were all that was keeping the enemy at bay. America was able to sleep, and go about their business, because the Jedi warriors of America were taking the fight to the enemy.

My own father taught his children the rich blessing this nation has to offer. He was a man who immigrated to the country from Italy, after having fought against the United States. He was fully embraced by his adopted country. I would always listen intently to the stories he spoke about how Fascism spread like a cancer in his country, eventually destroying his family, and leaving him orphaned at a young age with the death of his parents.

He enlisted in the Italian Navy during World War II; after the war had devastated his country—he immigrated to this country and began a new life. Starting a family, he would one day take them back to his country of origin, amazed at its transformation. All this happened because of the generous contribution of America and the will of its people to befriend a defeated foe.

America has always been the one indispensable nation willing to help all nations, whether friend or foe. All my life I could not wait to serve my country and was given the opportunity to serve as a United States Marine. During my time of service I had the unique opportunity to see the best of America: those serving in the armed forces of the United States.

While serving in Iraq and Afghanistan, I witnessed firsthand the charity and compassion of those Jedi warriors who at one moment were defeating the forces of darkness, and the next moment stretching forth a hand of compassion to those yearning to be free.

Now, it's my chance to let America know the quality of the men and women serving in the armed forces of this country and how this generation of Jedi warriors will re-shape America like the "Greatest Generation" re-shaped America and ushered in the greatest economic prosperity the world has ever known.

America today is besieged by partisan gridlock in Washington, a political and business elite more concerned with advancing its own power base than what is best for America. Far too often these elites look at America as what America can do for them instead what they can do for America.

Too often those who profess the spirit of President Kennedy fail to remember the axiom he stated in his inaugural address, "My fellow Americans: ask not what your country can do for you—ask what you can do for your country."

Too many Americans have forgotten this bold statement! Too many have failed to embrace his call to action, but the veterans of this country have not. As President Kennedy also stated, "In your hands, my fellow citizens, more than mine, will rest the final success or failure of our course. Since this country was founded, each generation of Americans has been summoned to give testimony to its national loyalty. The graves of young Americans who answered the call to service surround the globe."

Veterans remember their fallen comrades and will never diminish their legacy or tarnish their memory! Veterans will restore the honor and legacy of this great land, as the next "Greatest Generation" will re-shape America and again usher in an economic prosperity as President Reagan stated, "America's greatest days are not behind us but in front of us."

This country has a rendezvous with destiny, a destiny that is brighter than anything before and America will continue to lead her people into a bright future.

Unleash the power of the veterans of the United States Armed Forces!

ACKNOWLEDGEMENTS

This book is all about America's veterans and I wanted to give thanks for what they have provided, and continue to provide, for this country. The freedom we enjoy is because of the veterans who decided to serve their country and defend our way of life. Many members of the Armed Forces and all the units I served with in the United States Marines Corps helped shape who I am, and each duty assignment and position held in combat and peacetime had a profound effect on my career.

The Marine Corps has been my life for over thirty years and the Marine ethos has shaped who I am. I will always be a Marine physically and mentally. The challenges I have faced putting this book and my business together, and the skills I learned all have been learned because I served as a United States Marine.

The one individual who has been the most instrumental in helping me put this book together is Joe Yazbeck, owner of Prestige Leadership Advisors and best-selling author of *No Fear Speaking*. Joe Yazbeck took a veteran he saw at a business meeting and helped reshape his business and his life!

The transformation of Ubaldi Reports has been because of the guidance of Joe Yazbeck. Joe helped shape my thinking on how I should communicate, how I should address my audience, and how I should move my business forward. Joe was the one individual who helped put this book together. This book would not have been possible without his help, assistance, and guidance as a mentor to me, not only for Ubaldi Reports, but also in establishing the Vet Transition Academy—a place to help other veterans reach their goals! I am eternally grateful for the friendship and guidance Joe has provided.

Others who had a strong influence on me and my career include Major General James Williams (USMC-Ret) with whom I served in both Iraq and Afghanistan. His guidance in my endeavors helped shape my life by increasing my knowledge of the world around us and its impact on the United States. As a general officer in the Marines he was approachable and provided the strategic concepts I needed to fulfill my highest aspirations. General Williams is a Marine's Marine!

John and Cheryl Kennedy are two individuals who are more than just friends, they also have been mentors to me; they helped guide me and truly inspired me to reach my fullest potential. When I was at my lowest point, they were always there to help and assist me in any way possible. I can never thank John and Sheryl Kennedy enough! Tina and Russ Brown have been friends before I went to Iraq in 2005, and I look at them as family. They've always been there to help reassure me and assist me in anything I do. Nicky and Dennis Larson have also been my friends for years, and they are more than friends, something akin to a surrogate mother and father in guiding me to where I needed to go. I couldn't have done anything without them. Bill Rapaglia and John Wiegand, two men with whom I served in Afghanistan were both instrumental in instructing and mentoring me through the many difficulties and challenges of starting and growing a small business. Bill worked as a contractor in Afghanistan, but had served as a Marine in Vietnam. John was an army officer who taught and instructed me on military civil affairs. Both Bill and John advised me about moving my small business forward. Their help can never be calculated.

Jim and Meldra Clevenger have been there for me over the years, especially when I was pursuing my educational goals. They would inspire and guide me in my educational and business endeavors—even when I thought I had bitten off more than

I could chew. Both of them encouraged me to never quit if I wanted to reach my goals.

Dick and Judy Stoeltzing also had a profound impact on my life and helped shape it, guiding me to be a consistent voice not only for veterans but for all Americans with my company "Ubaldi Reports."

The members of my church, the Church of Jesus Christ of Latter Day Saints, all helped shape and support me while I was deployed in both Iraq and Afghanistan and became my biggest supporters with Ubaldi Reports.

Finally, even though they are no longer with me, I want to thank my parents who always pushed their children to reach their fullest potential. I know they were extremely proud of my service as a United States Marine, and the fact that I am a small business owner. My father, with only a grade school education, immigrated into this country and pushed his children to succeed. He always said, "If you want to succeed, you have to earn it. No one gives you something for nothing." My mother always told us to reach for the stars; she told us we can do anything we put our mind to. Without my parents I would not be the person I am today!

APPENDIX A

Top 100 Military Friendly Companies Listed by GI JOBS

1. USAA www.usaa.com

2. Union Pacific Railroad www.up.com

3. Verizon Communications Inc
   www.virizonwireless.com

4. CSX Corporation www.csx.com

5. ManTech International Corporation
   www.mantech.com

6. Combined Insurance Company of America
   www.combinedinsurance.com

7. Booz Allen Hamilton Inc www.boozallen.com

8. Southern Company www.southerncompany.com

9. Allied Barton Security Services
   www.Allied Barton.com

10. Schneider National, Inc www.schneider.com

11. General Electric Company www.ge.com

12. United Rentals www.unitedrentals.com

13. U-Haul International, Inc www.uhaul.com

14. J.B. Hunt Transport, Inc www.jbhunt.com

15. AT&T Inc www.att.com

16. Waste Management, Inc www.wm.com

17. Fugro www.fugro.com

18. Dyncorps International www.dyn-intl.com

19. Deloitte Federal www.deloitte.com

20. Gulf Stream Aerospace www.gulfstream.com

21. CACI International Inc www.caci.com

22. Ameren Corporation www.ameren.com

23. Dominion Resources, Inc www.dom.com

24. Capital One www.capitalone.com

25. PepsiCo, Inc www.pepsico.com

26. CDW www.cdw.com

27. JP Morgan Chase & Co www.jpmorgan.com

28. Fluor Corporation www.fluor.com

29. PSEG www.pseg.com

30. 7 Eleven www.7-eleven.com

31. The Home Depot Inc www.homedepot.com

32. Amazon.com, Inc www.amazon.com

33. G4S Secure Solutions (USA) www.g4s.us

34. Werner Enterprises Inc www.werner.com

35. Charles Schwab & Co., Inc www.schwab.com

36. Devon Energy Corporation www.devonenergy.com

37. Johnson Controls, Inc www.johnsoncontrols.com

38. CSC (Computer Sciences Corporation) www.csc.com

39. Sodexo www.sodexousa.com

40. State Farm www.statefarm.com

41. Qualcomm www.qualcomm.com

42. Merck & Co., Inc www.merk.com

43. Eaton Corporation www.eaton.com

44. ADS Inc www.adsinc.com

45. Northrop Grumman Corporation www.northropgrumman.com

46. Exelon Corporation www.exeloncorp.com

47. Burlington Northern Santa Fe www.bnsf.com

48. Xcel Energy www.xcelenergy.com

49. MidAmerican Energy www.midamericanenergy.com

50. Hewlett-Packard Company www.hp.com

51. PwC www.pwc.com

52. Corrections Corporation of America www.cca.com

53. DaVita, Inc www.davita.com

54. Crete Carrier Corporation www.cretecarrier.com

55. Engility Corporation www.engilitycorp.com

56. Bank of America Corporation
www.bankofamerica.com

57. U.S. Bank www.usbank.com

58. Sears Holdings Corporation www.searsholdings.com

59. Edward Jones www.edwardjones.com

60. Arizona Public Service www.aps.com

61. Chesapeake Energy Corporation www.chk.com

62. BAE Systems www.baesystems.com

63. Hormel Foods www.hormelfoods.com

64. The Western and Southern Life Insurance Company
www.westernsouthernlife.com

65. First Energywww.firstenergycorp.com

66. T-Mobile USA www.t-mobile.com

67. Walmart www.walmart.com

68. Penske Truck Leasing Co., L.P.
www.Pensketruckleasing.com

69. URS (Federal Services) www.urs.com

70. Southwest Airlines www.southwest.com

71. Prudential Financial www.prudential.com

72. United Health Group Inc www.unitedhealthgroup.com

73. Safeway Inc www.safeway.com

74. WellPoint, Inc www.wellpoint.com

75. Norfolk Southern Corporation www.nscorp.com

76. Comcast Corporation www.comcast.com

77. Patterson—UTI Drilling Company LLC www.patenergy.com

78. American Electric Power Company Inc www.aep.com

79. Baker Hughes Incorporated www.bakerhughes.com

80. Humana www.humana.com

81. Goodyear tire & Rubber Company www.goodyear.com

82. Siemens www.siemens.com

83. SAIC www.saic.com

84. Life Technologies www.lifetechnologies.com

85. Travelers www.travelers.com

86. Progressive Insurance www.progressive.com

87. Bechtel www.bechtel.com

88. Pacific Gas and Electric Company www.pge.com

89. Frontier Communications www.frontier.com

90. CINTAS Corporation www.cintas.com

91. General Mills www.generalmills.com

92. The GEO Group, Inc www.geogroup.com

93. Dollar General Corporation www.dollargeneral.com

94. Intel Corporation www.intel.com

95. Aviall Services Inc www.aviall.com

96. Citigroup Inc www.citigroup.com

97. Brink's U.S., A Division of Brink's, Incorporated www.us.brinksinc.com

98. CN-North America's Railroad www.cn.ca

99. Cubic Corporation www.cubic.com

100. Canadian Pacific Railroad www.cpr.ca

APPENDIX B

Top Veteran-Friendly Schools 2014 by U.S. Veterans Magazine

August 17, 2014 - 15:29

(Irvine, California) – August 15, 2014 – **The U.S. Veterans Magazine** today released the results of its much-anticipated 2014 evaluation of the nation's Best of the Best Top Veteran-Friendly Companies, Top Supplier Diversity Programs, Top VBOs and SDVBOs, Top Government & Law Enforcement Agencies and Top Veteran-Friendly Schools.

U.S. Veterans Magazine (USVM) polled hundreds of Fortune 1000 companies for this year's Best of the Best evaluations. At USVM, our goal is to open up employment, business and supplier opportunities within the federal government and corporate America for veterans, transitioning service members, disabled veterans, spouses and veteran business owners. The annual review is an evaluation of the nation's employers, initiatives, government agencies and educational institutions. These non-biased studies are valuable resources for job seekers, business owners, students, consumers, senior managers, business associations, employment agencies and consumer groups.

Congratulations to this year's winners, in alphabetical order:

1. American Military University

2. Angelo State University

3. Anne Arundel Community College

4.   Arizona State University

5.   Arkansas State University, Main Campus

6.   Ashford University

7.   Austin Peay State University

8.   Averett University

9.   Bellevue University

10. Berkeley College

11. Black Hills State University

12. Brandman University

13. Burlington County College

14. California State University San Marcos

15. California State University, San Bernardino

16. California University of Pennsylvania

17. Cameron University

18. Campbell University

19. Central Community College

20. Central Texas College

21. Chadron State College

22. Coleman University

23. Collin College

24. Columbia Southern University

25. Concord University

26. CUNY John Jay College of Criminal Justice

27. Cuyamaca College

28. Duquesne University

29. D'Youville College

30. Eastern Kentucky University

31. Embry-Riddle Aeronautical University

32. Erie Community College

33. Everest Colleges, Institutes & Universities

34. Excelsior

35. Fayetteville Technical Community College

36. Felician College

37. Florida Atlantic University

38. Florida Institute of Technology

39. Florida State University

40. Fordham University

41. Georgia Military College

42. Glendale Community College

43. Grantham University

44. Hanley Putnam University

45. Hawaii Pacific University

46. ICDC College

47. Indiana University-Purdue University

48. Irvine Valley College

49. Jones International University

50. Kaplan University,

51. Keiser University

52. Kennesaw State University

53. Liberty University,

54. Long Island University

55. Medaille College

56. Mercy College

57. Metropolitan State University of Denver

58. Middle Tennessee State University

59. Mississippi State University

60. MIT Sloan School of Management

61. Monmouth University West Long Branch, N.J.

62. Monroe Community College

63. Monterey Peninsula College

64. Montgomery College

65. Morehead State University

66. Mountwest Community & Technical College

67. Niagara University

68. North Lake College

69. Northern Arizona University

70. Northern Kentucky University

71. Northern Virginia Community College

72. Norwich University

73. Ohio State University

74. Old Dominion University

75. Oregon Institute of Technology

76. Ottawa University

77. Pasadena City College

78. Post University

79. ed Rocks Community College

80. Richard Stockton College of New Jersey

81. Rutgers, The State University of New Jersey

82. Salt Lake Community College

83. San Diego State University

84. Shoreline Community College

85. Solano Community College

86. South Dakota School of Mines and Technology

87. South Dakota State University

88. Southern Illinois University Carbondale

89. St. Petersburg College

90. Stratford University

91. SUNY College at Plattsburgh

92. Texas A&M University

93. Texas A&M University-San Antonio

94. Texas State University

95. Texas Tech University

96. Thomas Edison State College

97. Troy University

98. The George Washington University

99. The Ohio State University

100. The University of Oklahoma, Norman Campus

101. The University of Texas at Arlington

102. The University of Texas at Austin

103. The University of Texas at El Paso

104. The University of Texas at Tyler

105. Thomas Edison State College

106. Tidewater Community College

107. Towson University

108. Troy University

109. University of Alabama

110. University of California, Berkeley

111. University of California, Los Angeles

112. University of Colorado Denver

113. University of Evansville,

114. University of Georgia

115. Terry College of Business MBA Program

116. University of Kansas

117. University of Kentucky

118. University of Maine at Augusta

119. University of Massachusetts Lowell

120. University of Michigan

121. University of Missouri, Columbia

122. University of Nebraska

123. University of New Haven

124. University of Northern Iowa

125. University of North Georgia

126. University of Phoenix

127. University of South Dakota

128. University of Southern California Marshall School of Business

129. University of South Florida

130. University of the Incarnate Word

131. University of West Florida

132. University West Long Branch, N.J.

133. University of Wisconsin Oshkosh

134. University of Wisconsin-Eau Claire

135. University of Wisconsin-River Falls

136. Vanguard University of Southern California

137. Virginia Western Community College

138. Webster University

139. Western Illinois University

140. Western Kentucky University

141. Western Michigan University

142. Western Nebraska Community College

143. West Virginia University

144. Wright State University

145. WyoTech

WORKS CITED

INTRODUCTION

Chaplain, Mike. *InternetMonk.com.* November 11, 2010. http://www.internetmonk.com/archive/13674 (accessed September 07, 2014).

Fraser, Alan. "An Extraordinary Speech." *American Thinker,* December 12, 2010.

Gates, Robert. *Duty Memoirs of a Secretary At War.* New York City: Random House, 2014. Pg 592-593

Maffucci, Jacqueline. *Iraq Afghanistan Veterans of America.* August 01, 2014. http://iava.org/blog/veteran-unemployment-rate-increases-June (accessed September 07, 2014).

Office, United State Government Accountability. *Transitioning Veterans Improved Oversight Needed to Enhance Implementation of Transition Assistance Program.* GAO Report to Congressional Committees, Washington D.C.: U.S. Federal Government, March 2014.

http://www.va.gov/budget/docs/summary/Fy2015-FastFactsVAsBudgetHighlights.pdf

SECTION ONE

Affairs, U.S. Department of Veteran. *U.S. department of Veteran Affairs.* n.d. http://www.benefits.va.gov/gibill/history.asp (accessed September 10, 2014).

Christensen, Lt Col Dave Grossman with Loren W. *On combat The Psychology of Deadly Conflict in War and Peace.* Washington D.C.: Warrior Science Publications, 2004, 2007, 2008.

Greengard, Samuel. *Workforce.com.* February 22, 2012. http://www.workforce.com/articles/fighting-for-employment-veterans-in-the-40s-and-today (accessed September 10, 2014).

Military.com. *Military.com.* n.d. http://www.military.com/veteran-jobs/career-advice/military-transition/veterans-in-college-face-challenges.html (accessed September 10, 2014).

SECTION TWO

Gavett, Gretchen. *Harvard Business Review.* March 24, 2014. http://blogs.hbr.org/2014/03/what-military-service-could-teach-mbas/ (accessed September 09, 2014).

Obama, First Lady Michelle. *WhiteHouse.gov.* April 17, 2013. http://www.whitehouse.gov/the-press-office/2013/04/17/remarks-first-lady-veterans-full-employment-act-2013-bill-signing (accessed September 08, 2014).

Obama, President Barrack. *Whitehouse.gov.* June 01, 2012. http://www.whitehouse.gov/the-press-office/2012/06/01/remarks-president-veterans-jobs-golden-valley-minnesota (accessed September 08, 2014).

Quinton, Sophie. *National Journal.* September 11, 2013. http://www.nationaljournal.com/next-economy/solutions-bank/why-are-companies-reluctant-to-hire-military-veterans-20130911 (accessed September 08, 2014).

Reynolds Lewis, Katherine. *3 Reasons why companies Don't hire Veterans.* November 11, 2013. http://fortune.com/2013/11/11/3-reasons-why-companies-dont-hire-veterans/ (accessed September 08, 2014).

Fortune. November 11, 2013. http://fortune.com/2013/11/11/3-reasons-why-companies-dont-hire-veterans/ (accessed September 08, 2014).

Robinson, Shane. *Forbes.* August 12, 2013. http://www.forbes.com/sites/shanerobinson/2013/08/12/why-a-veteran-might-be-your-next-best-hire/ (accessed September 09, 2014).

SECTION THREE

Alden, Edward. *Council on Foreign Relations.* June 26, 2012. http://blogs.cfr.org/renewing-america/2012/06/26/foreign-languages-and-u-s-economic-competitiveness/ (accessed September 09, 2014).

Commerce, University Colorado Denver & Denver Metro Chamber of. *University Colorado Denver & Denver Metro Chamber of Commerce.* 2014. http://www.ucdenver.edu/about/WhoWeAre/community/boots-to-suits/Pages/TopTenReasonsToHireVeteran.aspx (accessed September 09, 2014).

SECTION FOUR

Citroen, Lida. *Entrepreneur.* July 21, 2014. http://www.entrepreneur.com/article/235754 (accessed September 09, 2014).

Company, Syracuse University and Mackenzie and. *How Companies Can Capture the Veteran Opportunity.* September 11, 2012. http://toolkit.vets.syr.edu/wp-content/uploads/2012/11/Presentation-1-20120911-Veteran-opportunity.pdf (accessed September 09, 2014).

Families, Syracuse University Institute for Veterans and Military. *"The Business Case for Hiring a Veteran Beyond the Cliches".* March 5, 2012. http://www.dol.gov/vets/vrap/Syracuse%20Business%20Case%20to%20Hire%20a%20Vet.pdf (accessed September 09, 2014).

Magazine, *U.S. Veterans. U.S. Veterans Magazine.* August 17, 2014. http://www.usveteransmagazine.com/article/top-veteran-friendly-schools-2014 (accessed September 09, 2014).

Smith, Jacquelyn. *Forbes Magazine.* November 11, 2013. http://www.forbes.com/sites/jacquelynsmith/2013/11/11/top-military-friendly-employers/ (accessed September 09, 2014).

SECTION FIVE

O'Donnell. *Why do Veterans Make the Best Entrepreneurs.* April 25, 2014. http://www.wjla.com/articles/2014/04/why-do-veterans-make-the-best-entrepreneurs--102503.html (accessed September 09, 2014).

Singer, Dan Senor & Saul. *Start Up Nation The Story of Israel's Economic Miracle.* New York City: Hachette Book Group, 2009.

Weiss, Geoff. *Entrepreneur Magazine.* May 23, 2014. http://www.entrepreneur.com/article/234143 (accessed September 10, 2014).

SECTION SIX

Feaver, Peter D. *ForeignPolicy.com.* May 13, 2014. http://shadow.foreignpolicy.com/posts/2014/05/12/it_matters_when_the_military_engages_civilian_elites (accessed September 10, 2014).

Kennedy, Lt Gen Karl Eikenberry & David. *"Americans and Their Military, Drifting Apart" New York Times.* May 26, 2013. http://www.nytimes.com/2013/05/27/opinion/americans-and-their-military-drifting-apart.html?pagewanted=all&_r=0 (accessed September 10, 2014).

Manning, Jennifer E. *Congressional Research Service: Membership of the 113th Congress: A Profile.* July 14, 2014. http://fas.org/sgp/crs/misc/R42964.pdf (accessed September 10, 2014).

Mansoor, Col Peter R. *Baghdad at Sunrise.* Yale, CT : Yale Library of Military History , 2008.

Raasch, Chuck. *St Louis Post Dispatch.* May 26, 2014. http://www.stltoday.com/news/local/govt-and-politics/number-of-veterans-in-congress-has-fallen-drastically-since-post/article_bd824d5f-0a02-569c-91fc-0b7a62b6dab1.html (accessed September 26, 2014).

Skelton, Ike. *Joint Forces Quarterly.* 1st Quarter 2012. http://www.huschblackwell.com/~/media/Files/BusinessInsights/BusinessInsights/2012/01/The%20CivilMilitary%20Gap%20Need%20Not%20Become%20a%20Chasm%20em__/Files/The%20Civil-Military%20Gap%20Need%20Not%20Become%20a%20Chasm/FileAttachment/Civ-MilGapJFQ1-2012 (Accessed September 10, 2014).

USMC, Lieutenant General John F. Kelly. *American Thinker.* December 12, 2010. Lieutenant General John F. Kelly USMC (accessed September 10, 2014).

Rein, Lisa. *Washington Post.* September 15, 2014. http://www.washingtonpost.com/politics/obama-push-to-hire-veterans-into-federal-jobs-spurs-resentment/2014/09/14/c576e592-2edc-11e4-bb9b-997ae96fad33_story.html (accessed September 15, 2014).

Williams, Rudi. *U.S. Department of Defense.* November 10, 2003. http://www.defense.gov/news/newsarticle.aspx?id=27819 (accessed September 16, 2014).

SECTION SEVEN

Groat, Arthur S. De. *Looking Critically at Reintegration of Post 9-11 Era Military Veterans.* 2013. http://www.k-state.edu/militaryaffairs/docs/Reintegrating-Post-9-11-Military-Veterans.pdf (accessed September 11, 2014).

Harrell, Nancy Berglass & Margaret C. *Center for a New American Security.* April 2012. http://www.cnas.org/files/documents/publications/CNAS_WellAfterService_BerglassHarrell.pdf (accessed September 11, 2014).

Morin, Rich. *Pew Research Social & Demographic Trends.* December 8, 2011. http://www.pewsocialtrends.org/2011/12/08/ the-difficult-transition-from-military-to-civilian-life (accessed September 11, 2014).

Trends, Pew Research Social & Demographic. *Pew Research Social & Demographic Trends.* October 5, 2011. http://www. pewsocialtrends.org/2011/10/05/war-and-sacrifice-in-the-post-911-era (accessed September 11, 2014).

SECTION EIGHT

Axelrod, Jim. *CBS News.* May 2014, 2014. http://www. cbsnews.com/news/vas-overmedication-of-vets-widespread-in-spector-general-finds (accessed September 13, 2014).

Axelrod, Jim. *CBS News.* September 19, 2013. http://www. cbsnews.com/news/veterans-dying-from-overmedication (accessed September 13, 2014).

Berglass, Margaret C. Harrell & Nancy. *Center for New America Security.* June 2012. http://www.cnas.org/sites/default/ files/publications-pdf/CNAS_EmployingAmericasVeterans_ HarrellBerglass.pdf (accessed September 13, 2014).

Callaghan, Marty. *The American Legion.* May 02, 2014. http://www.legion.org/veteransbenefits/221942/legion-testi-fies-va-over-medication-issue (accessed September 13, 2014).

Carter, Phillip. *Portland Press Herald.* April 8, 2014. http:// www.pressherald.com/2014/04/08/commentary__ptsd_is_a_ big_concern_for_veterans__but_their_whole_story_is_more_ complex_/ (accessed September 13, 2014).

Collins, Senator Susan. *Website of Senator Susan Collins.* June 04, 2013. http://www.collins.senate.gov/public/index. cfm/2013/6/senators-introduce-bipartisan-legislation-to-cre-ate-prescription-drug-take-back-system-for-vets (accessed September 13, 2014).

Fraser, Alan. *American Thinker.* December 12, 2010. http://www.americanthinker.com/2010/12/an_extraordinary_speech.html (accessed September 13, 2014).

Gade, Daniel. *National Affairs.* Summer 2013. http://www.nationalaffairs.com/publications/detail/a-better-way-to-help-veterans (accessed September 13, 2014).

Glantz, Aaron. *The Center for Investigative Reporting.* September 28, 2013. http://cironline.org/reports/vas-opiate-overload-feeds-veterans-addictions-overdose-deaths-5261 (accessed September 13, 2014).

Grossman, Lt Col Dave. *On combat The Psychology and Physiology of Deadly Conflict in war and Peace.* Washington D.C.: Warrior Science Publication, 2004, 2007, 2008.

Karen H. Seal, MD, MPH, et al. *The Journal of the American Medical Association.* March 7, 2012. https://jama.jamanetwork.com/article.aspx?articleid=1105046#ArticleInformation (accessed September 13, 2014).

Mansoor, Col Peter. *Baghdad at Sunris, A Brigade commander's War in Iraq.* New Haven, CT: Yale University Press, 2008.

Mientka, Matthew. *Medical Daily.com.* November 12, 2013. http://www.medicaldaily.com/veterans-administration-accused-over-medicating-war-veterans-many-now-battling-addiction-along-pain (accessed September 13, 2014).

Owens, Mackubin Thomas. *Weekly Standard.* June 2, 2014. http://www.weeklystandard.com/articles/life-after-wartime_793486.html (accessed September 13, 2014).

Zoroya, Gregg. *USA Today.* April 09, 2013. http://www.usatoday.com/story/news/nation/2013/04/06/recent-war-vets-face-hiring-obstacle-ptsd-bias/2057857 (accessed September 13, 2014).

SECTION NINE

(TMC), The Military Coalition. *Senate Armed Services Subcommittee on Personnel.* March 26, 2014. http://www.armed-services.senate.gov/imo/media/doc/TMC_Testimony_03-26-14.pdf (accessed September 13, 2014).

Lauren Everitt, Andrew Theen and Gulnaz Saiyed. *Washington Post.* February 14, 201. http://www.washingtonpost.com/national/national-security/efforts-lag-to-improve-care-for-national-guard/2012/02/04/gIQAymEWER_story.html (accessed September 13, 2014).

Torreon, Lawarence Kapp & Barbara Salazar. *Congressional Research Service.* June 13, 2014. http://fas.org/sgp/crs/natsec/RL30802.pdf (accessed September 13, 2014)

ABOUT THE AUTHOR

JOHN UBALDI, USMC Ret. is a 30-year veteran of the United States Marine Corps who completed three combat tours in Iraq and Afghanistan. During his time in the Marine Corps, John became one of the foremost authorities on Civil Affairs as it relates to Counterinsurgency and Irregular Warfare. With his knowledge of Middle Eastern Culture and National Security policy, he appeared on a number of news programs including the syndicated, *Washington Journal.* As an author, he has written articles for various military journals.

Witnessing firsthand the high degree of poverty and devastation in the Middle East as a marine, John personally organized $6 million dollars in humanitarian aid to Iraq and Afghanistan, as well as to other nations around the globe, including Thailand, Nicaragua, and the Philippines. He received his B.A. in government from California State University in Sacramento, and an

M.A. in National Security Studies with a concentration in Middle Eastern Studies from the American Military University.

John is also the founder of Ubaldi Reports, a Media publishing company which provides credible, political content, addressing domestic and global issues giving the United States more knowledgeable and responsible citizens.

www.ubaldireports.com
john@ubaldireports.com

813-415-3048

CPSIA information can be obtained
at www.ICGtesting.com
Printed in the USA
LVOW04s0220080316

478209LV00018B/263/P